CAPE TOWN
THE CITY AT A GLANCE

Company's Garden
Planted by the Dutch East India C[ompany in]
1652, the tree-lined public park is [flanked]
by museums and government ins[titutions.]

Robben Island
Nelson Mandela was an inmate at this political
prison, which has been turned into a museum.

Cape Town Stadium
Built for the 2010 World Cup, the eye-catching
arena hosts sporting events and big gigs.
See p014

City Hall
The 1905 Edwardian pile, the site of Mandela's
first post-release speech, is now a culture hub.
Darling Street, T 021 444 7518

V&A Waterfront
It's super touristy, but the Watershed artisan
market and MOCAA (see p030) are proper hits.

Railway Station
Opened in 1863 and revamped in 1965, the
station has glass mosaics and terrazzo eaves.
Adderley Street

Castle of Good Hope
William Fehr's collection of decorative arts
makes this 1679 fortress worth a visit.
See p009

Civic Centre
Councillors convene below the brutalist slab
in a podium building with a shuttlecock roof.
See p086

District Six
After the 1966 Group Areas Act, the multiracial
working-class community here was resettled.
Scars of the past are evident in its vacant plots.

INTRODUCTION
THE CHANGING FACE OF THE URBAN SCENE

Due to Cape Town's jaw-dropping setting below Table Mountain, one of the world's natural wonders, its miles of unspoilt coast and winelands for suburbs, you could fall for the place on looks alone. But this obscures the fact that it is also smoothly functional, with a thriving financial district and a robust streak of can-do energy that drives local creativity, and over the past two decades it has emerged as a vibrant destination for cuisine, design and contemporary art.

There's an abundance of modish bars and cafés, and exceptional fine dining, with waves of eateries and galleries colonising the CBD, in particular along Bree Street, and in summer, the upscale beach enclaves of Camps Bay and Clifton turn into South Africa's de facto party haunts. Woodstock, historically the country's workshop, has morphed into an arts hub, and even the sterile V&A Waterfront, once simply a glorified mall, is now worth a visit for its cultural offerings. Among all this, there is a plethora of accommodation options, from remnants of white-mischief colonial grandeur to stunning private rentals; indeed, much of the domestic architecture here is peerless.

Yet for all its abundant beauty, signs of inequality are depressingly plentiful. The city is fringed by squalid ghettos, stark reminders of apartheid, and walking its streets requires some caution, especially after dark and in the wilds. However, this gritty edginess coexists with a palpable optimism born of the belief that Cape Town is truly heading in the right direction. It is a ride you shouldn't miss.

ESSENTIAL INFO
FACTS, FIGURES AND USEFUL ADDRESSES

TOURIST OFFICE
Pinnacle Building
Burg Street/Castle Street
T 086 132 2223
www.capetown.travel

TRANSPORT
Airport transfer to city centre
The shuttle bus takes roughly 30 minutes
www.myciti.org.za
Car hire
Drive Africa
T 021 447 1144
Helicopter
Civair
T 021 934 4488
Taxis
Excite Taxis
T 021 448 4444
Ride-hailing services are ubiquitous but if in doubt call for a registered taxi

EMERGENCY SERVICES
Emergencies
T 107 (from a landline)
T 021 480 7700 (from a mobile)
Late-night pharmacy (until 11pm)
Lite-kem Pharmacy
24 Darling Street
T 021 461 8040

CONSULATES
British Consulate General
15th floor, Norton Rose House
8 Riebeek Street
T 021 405 2400
www.gov.uk/world/south-africa
US Consulate General
2 Reddam Avenue
Westlake
T 021 702 7300
za.usembassy.gov

POSTAL SERVICES
Post office
Loop Street/Pepper Street
T 021 424 7477
Shipping
DHL
T 086 034 5000

BOOKS
Cape Town: A City Imagined edited by
Stephen Watson (Penguin)
Modern Wineries of South Africa
by Hugh Fraser (Quivertree)

WEBSITES
Architecture
www.futurecapetown.com
Art/Design
www.10and5.com
www.artthrob.co.za
www.designindaba.com
Newspaper
www.dailymaverick.co.za

EVENTS
Art Week
www.artweek.co.za
First Thursdays
www.first-thursdays.co.za

COST OF LIVING
Taxi from Cape Town International Airport to city centre
R300
Cappuccino
R28
Packet of cigarettes
R40
Daily newspaper
R9
Bottle of champagne
R700

CAPE TOWN
Population
4 million
Currency
Rand
Telephone codes
South Africa: 27
Cape Town: 021
Local time
GMT +2
Flight time
London: 12 hours

AVERAGE TEMPERATURE / °C

AVERAGE RAINFALL / MM

NEIGHBOURHOODS
THE AREAS YOU NEED TO KNOW AND WHY

To help you navigate the city, we've chosen the most interesting districts (see below and the map inside the back cover) and colour-coded our featured venues, according to their location; those venues that are outside these areas are not coloured.

ATLANTIC SEABOARD
The slopes of super-suburbs Camps Bay and Clifton are crowded with modernist villas and buzzy haunts like the evergreen Caprice (37 Victoria Road, T 021 438 8315). Bantry Bay and Fresnaye are also chichi, if more solidly residential. Sea Point is the poor cousin but has trusty delis including Kleinsky's (95 Regent Road, T 021 433 2871) and a delightful promenade (see p027). The sunsets are straight out of central casting.

GREEN POINT
A hulking yet graceful sports stadium (see p014) now defines Green Point, although its louche cafés and bars continue to be the draw for locals. De Waterkant, formerly a Cape Malay neighbourhood, has a vibrant gay culture, and ritzy lifestyle boutiques cluster around the upscale Cape Quarter precinct (27 Somerset Road, T 021 421 1111). Granger Bay, once a rather forlorn outpost, is home to Grand Africa Café & Beach (see p047), a hideaway from the urban bustle.

CENTRE
An artery leading from the harbour up the mountain, Long Street has an edgy boho vibe, and is a nightlife hub. Bree Street, which runs parallel, is the dining strip du jour (see p026). Church Street intersects both and has a number of quality galleries (see p078). To the west is Bo-Kaap, a Cape Malay area known for its colourful houses and boutiques. Digital whizz-kids add to the creative mix in gentrifying East City.

WATERFRONT/LOWER CITY
The V&A Waterfront, a successful and safe entertainment complex, is one of the city's proudest moments, although its Disneyfied Victoriana soon grates. Skip the mall, skim the craft stalls at the Watershed (see p091) and peruse art and design at MOCAA (see p030) and Southern Guild (see p068). In Lower City, the Civic Centre (see p086) and Artscape theatre (DF Malan Street, T 021 410 9800) form a fine brutalist ensemble.

WOODSTOCK
It may still be rough around the edges and can become sketchy after dark, but some of South Africa's best commercial galleries, in particular Stevenson and Goodman (see p065), are found in and around Sir Lowry Road. Running parallel, Albert Road is now a design destination (see p088). Also look out for murals by Faith XLVII (see p074) and DALeast. The Test Kitchen (see p050) and La Bottega (160 Sir Lowry Road, T 021 461 9731) are stalwarts of frontier dining.

CITY BOWL SUBURBS
Set on the lower reaches of Table Mountain and Signal Hill, des-res Gardens, Vredhoek, Tamboerskloof, Oranjezicht and Higgovale are dotted with boutique hotels (see p022) and architect-designed villas. Kloof Street is lined with emporiums like Olive Branch Deli (see p062), daytime hangouts, such as Café Paradiso (No 110, T 021 422 0403), which has a garden setting, and laidback eateries, typified by Black Sheep (see p051).

LANDMARKS
THE SHAPE OF THE CITY SKYLINE

Elsewhere in the world you might navigate by skyscrapers, bridges and parks, but here nothing can compete with the kilometre-high rock that is bang in the middle of the city. Perversely, it can be disorientating. On the ground, it's hard to grasp that much of Cape Town is on the other side of one peak or another. In the City Bowl, nestled in the crook of Table Mountain (see p025) and Lion's Head, you feel as if you are in a small town. Then you nip over Kloof Nek and the Atlantic Seaboard is revealed, with its beachside hamlets and a dozen more peaks, the Twelve Apostles, reaching along the coast. Scoot around the back and suburbs stretch past Newlands (and its beautiful cricket ground), all the way to False Bay.

The city is not without manmade landmarks. The Castle of Good Hope (Castle Street, T 021 787 1260), a squat 1679 pentagon, marks the old seafront before the Foreshore was reclaimed from Mother Nature in the 1930s. The area is now home to the high-rises that define the CBD. There's the monumental vacancy of District Six, a multiracial quarter that was bulldozed during apartheid and is being gradually transformed into affordable housing. Standing out, however, are structures that have become enduring symbols almost in spite of themselves: the love-them or loathe-them Disa Park Towers (overleaf), the retro-futurist Ritz Hotel (see p013) and the perfectly situated Cape Town Stadium (see p014).

For full addresses, see Resources.

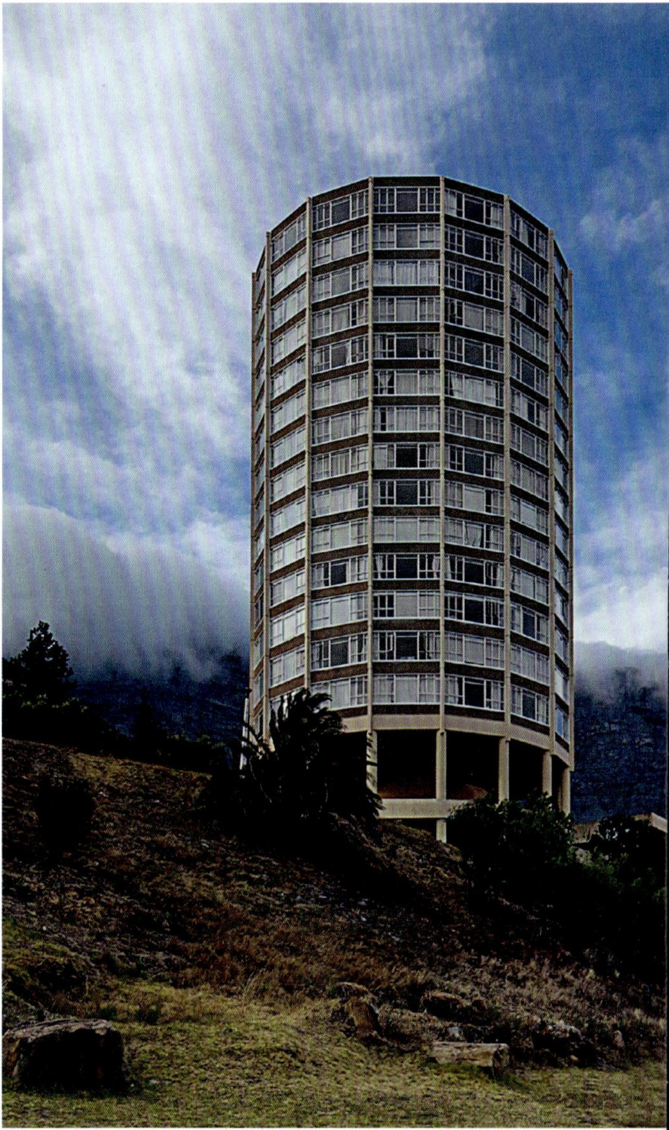

Disa Park Towers
Unfairly nicknamed the Tampon Towers, this trio of multistorey 1960s apartment blocks is an eyesore to some and an icon to others. Conceived by construction firm Murray & Roberts on the slopes of Table Mountain, their height was controversial, and the summer southeaster, notoriously strong here, exacts its revenge. Shelter at The Sidewalk Café (T 021 461 2839). *Chelmsford Road*

Zeitz MOCAA / The Silo

Designed by Brit Thomas Heatherwick and named after German Jochen Zeitz, whose African art collection it houses, you'd be forgiven for wondering how Saffers figure in this ambitious scheme. Prominently, as it turns out. The project was initiated by the V&A Waterfront, which is co-owned by the huge state pension fund, and three local architectural firms assisted Heatherwick in his steampunk transformation of these 1920s grain silos into a nine-floor museum (see p030) topped by a hotel, distinctive for its bulging, faceted windows. It launched with a real fanfare in 2017. Many industrial elements have been incorporated, like the railway tracks and conveyor system at the entrance, while Michele Mathison's nearby sculpture is made from five iron flywheels that powered the original elevators.
S Arm Road, www.zeitzmocaa.museum

Ritz Hotel

A jaded tower with a UFO on top, the Ritz is not very ritzy these days. It opened in 1970, a time of great prosperity for white South Africans, as an upscale address known for its tinkly piano ambience. It rises, almost embarrassed, above Sea Point's Victorian, Edwardian and modern residences, yet is far and away the most interesting building in the district, although it is not the tallest in town – that honour belongs to the 136m Portside in the CBD, finished in 2014. Time has not been kind to this veteran, cruelly dubbed the Pitz. There have been attempts to revive its faded glamour; in 2018, a judge dismissed a failed makeover as 'chutzpah of the first order'. But the 2019 arrival of The Glengariff, a condo and mall next door, signalled a possible return to grace for the hotel and its revolving rooftop restaurant.
Main Road/Camberwell Road

Cape Town Stadium

German practice GMP worked with Cape Town architects Louis Karol and Point to create this saucer-like oval, its glinting facade of woven fibreglass coated with Teflon. Its finest moment came in 2010 when 64,100 people witnessed Germany embarrass Diego Maradona's Argentina 4-0 in the FIFA World Cup quarter-final. The capacity has been reduced to 55,000 and it now serves as the home ground of two local football teams, and hosts rugby matches and touring megastars. Many still question why a whopping R4.5bn was lavished on this folly, which is visible from much of the city, in light of far more pressing social issues, although it has led to upgrades of the area, including an eco park. Happily, legendary deli Giovanni's (T 021 434 6893) is still going strong.
Fritz Sonnenberg Road

LANDMARKS

HOTELS

WHERE TO STAY AND WHICH ROOMS TO BOOK

The film and fashion packs' love affair with photogenic Cape Town endures, and the accommodation that has sprung up to house them will satisfy the diva in all of us. Bear in mind that location is crucial because the city is sectioned by its topography. If you're based on the Atlantic coast, for instance, it's tiresome to keep crossing Kloof Nek to get to the City Bowl. Splitting your stay with a central stint as well as a beachy spot like The Marly (201 Victoria Road, T 021 437 1287), with its Grecian white suites, is an ideal solution.

If you're a room-service addict, book the Belmond Mount Nelson (76 Orange Street, T 021 483 1000), a Victorian institution moulded into an African Claridge's, revamped by Inge Moore in 2017. On the same tip, on the V&A Waterfront, there's the funky The Silo (Silo Square, T 021 670 0500) and stately Cape Grace (West Quay Road, T 021 410 7100). Many boutique properties offer a personal touch, notably Ellerman House (see p019), POD (see p020) and 2inn1 Kensington (21 Kensington Crescent, T 021 423 1707), in Higgovale.

Some of the best places to stay are bijou rentals: the rooms with wraparound balconies at 26 Sunset Villa (26 Sunset Avenue, T 082 826 9986) above a cove in Llandudno, The Penthouse at Glen Beach Bungalow (12 Glen Beach, T 083 675 8266), and 21 Nettleton (21 Nettleton Road, T 021 438 1122), six suites within a hillside mansion. There really is no substitute for having your very own address.
For full addresses and room rates, see Resources.

Gorgeous George

This hotel straddles two adjacent heritage properties, one of them Edwardian and the other art deco. For its 2019 launch, Urbane Citizen Architecture's renovation preserved original features such as the cornices and architraves, while exposing the concrete skeleton to instil a contemporary aesthetic. Tristan du Plessis' interiors are a showcase of native creativity. The 32 rooms feature Gregor Jenkin's 'Quaker' chairs and Douglas & Company's 'McSorley's Wonderful Saloon' bar trolleys, as well as hand-painted murals by artist David Brits. The hues of Lucie De Moyencourt's 1,800-tile delftware-style city map in the lobby are echoed in the rugs in the Studios (above). Head to the sixth-floor terrace for late-afternoon grazing and drinks at Gigi Rooftop and a dip in the pool.
118 St George's Mall, T 087 898 6000,
www.gorgeousgeorge.co.za

Camps Bay Retreat

Less than a century ago, Camps Bay was a rustic getaway for Capetonians on a slow tram, a draw for its breezes and tin beach huts. That all changed in 1929 when mine owner Friedrich Wilhelm Knacke employed local architect William Grant to design an Edwardian manor house situated on a bluff between ravines. The venue is now made up of two next-door properties, the Afro-modern Deck House as well as the original residence, which remains the crown jewel. Out of the 19 rooms, the four here come in classic Cape colonial style; opt for Room One for its marble art deco bathroom and three balconies, one of which faces Lion's Head. The private reserve has a spa and tennis courts, and a path through stone pines leads to a hillside meditation pool.
7 Chilworth Road, T 021 437 8300,
www.campsbayretreat.com

Ellerman House

Once the summer retreat of the shipping magnate Sir John Ellerman and his wife, this Cape Edwardian mansion has been transformed into the preferred address of film stars and royalty by its art-loving owner, financier Paul Harris. Positioned on a sloping site in Bantry Bay, known for its huge granite boulders, Ellerman House proffers 13 rooms individually finished in mostly classic rather than contemporary styles; we suggest splurging on one of the villas. The main bedroom (above) at Villa One has sliding doors that open out onto a wooden balcony overlooking the ocean. Villa Two comprises three bedrooms and perches above a 7,500-bottle wine cellar that was part-designed by sculptor Angus Taylor. There is also an excellent gallery.
180 Kloof Road, T 021 430 3200, www.ellerman.co.za

POD

Above Camps Bay beach, this fastidiously rectilinear creation designed by architect Greg Wright is a charmer. Less clunky than many of the wood-and-steel copycats seen nearby, the svelte 17-room boutique hotel is distinguished by its open-plan interior and synthesis of straightforward raw materials (walls of stone and oak) with high-quality furnishings. The Balconies in the Deluxe Suites (above) enable you to observe the body-conscious practising yoga on the sand below, although you might well prefer the ocean view from the bar/lounge. Note that staying in this part of town does require a certain affinity to people traffic, especially in the summer, when the restaurants, bars and clubs are regularly jam-packed. POD's king-sized beds offer ample reprieve.
3 Argyle Street, T 021 438 8550, www.pod.co.za

HOTELS

Kensington Place

The howling summer wind rarely disturbs protected Higgovale, the architecturally daring City Bowl suburb where this chic nine-suite hotel is situated. Compared to its flashy neighbours, Kensington Place looks almost Calvinist, which is not to say it isn't homely. The individually appointed rooms meld slick decorative touches and pieces by local artists including Zwelethu Mthethwa and Stephen Inggs, and there are unspoilt panoramas from the balconies. Public spaces are a little more lavish, with copper panelling behind the reception and a velvet banquette in the lounge helping to evoke a tranquil Zanzibar mood. There is also a sheltered garden and pool (above). Seemingly set below Table Mountain, the residence is only a stroll from Kloof Street. *38 Kensington Crescent, T 021 424 4744, www.kensingtonplace.co.za*

The Tree House Boutique Hotel
Secreted on Signal Hill above the harbour, this bucolic retreat was designed by local architect Gerd Weideman and opened in 2017. Its 14 rooms either face the mountain or the Atlantic (we recommend the upper-level sea-view options) and have calming interiors by Yolanda Le Roux — subdued tones of smoky grey, olive and sand, and warm furnishings. Many of these pieces have been produced by city firms, such as the 'Cart-on 1' pendant lights by Spazio (above, in the Superior Mountain Room); Indigi Designs' 'Fracture Armchair'; and salvaged-wood cabinets in the breakfast area, which looks out onto a secluded pool. There's also art by Capetonians, including charcoal drawings by Kendall-Leigh Nash and Cathy Layzell's colourist paintings.
28 Vesperdene Road, T 021 439 9296, www.thetreehouseboutiquehotel.co.za

24 HOURS

SEE THE BEST OF THE CITY IN JUST ONE DAY

Cape Town can please and tease you for a week and still leave you wanting more. If you're short on time, focus on what the city does best – food and wine in a resplendent natural setting. Capetonians are early risers: join them for a pre-breakfast ride up Table Mountain (opposite) for superb views, and once you've refuelled (see p026), have a reviving dip at Sea Point (see p027). En route to the National Gallery (see p028), nose around Sir Herbert Baker's St George's Cathedral (5 Wale Street, T 021 424 7360) and load up on caffeine at The Company's Garden Restaurant (15 Queen Victoria Street, T 021 423 2919), sat in a Porky Hefer (see p068) outdoor nest.

Our ambitious itinerary includes a trip to Stellenbosch; take the N1 to pass the Taal Monument (see p032) on the way to the wine estates Delaire Graff (see p034) and Tokara (Helshoogte Pass, T 021 808 5900). Or you might prefer to head down the Cape Peninsula to Muizenberg for a surf, or to bask on Bakoven Beach. Even if you don't catch a performance at Baxter Theatre (see p036), pop by its Long Bar for a snifter. And afterwards, dine on antelope in barberry jus at Aubergine (39 Barnet Street, T 021 465 0000), or the lauded fusion dishes at Liam Tomlin's Chefs Warehouse & Canteen (92 Bree Street, T 021 422 0128). Then dive into the late-night melee at hip bars Hank's Olde Irish (110 Bree Street, T 021 422 2770) and Orphanage Cocktail Emporium (227 Bree Street, T 071 534 0266). *For full addresses, see Resources.*

07.00 Table Mountain

Pilots cruise past Table Mountain (sit on the right on most flights arriving into Cape Town) and it dominates every vista of the city. The cloud that often shrouds its flat top in summer is known as the Tablecloth, but if the weather's clear, head up for the sunrise. At 1,085m, it's a tough trek – go equipped and accompanied, as an urban mountain is no safer than any other. Or buy tickets online (there's often a long queue at the booth) for the five-minute journey in one of the Swiss-designed cable cars, which began running in 1997 after an upgrade of the 1929 Aerial Cableway (T 021 424 8181; check operating times). The floors of the pods revolve, affording 360-degree views. There is a self-service café at the summit, though we'd advise you to bring provisions from Peppertree Café (T 021 424 5540) on Kloof Street, and a crisp sauvignon blanc.

08.00 Between Us

Twins Jesse and Jamie Friedberg built their reputation at Skinny Legs (T 021 423 5403) and started over in 2018 with this bistro in a pair of refurbished Victorian properties. Familiar traditions endure: Jamie still runs the kitchen and Jesse doles out smiles front of house. The dining area features original sandstone walls bound with white cement; the kiaat furniture was made by locals Tinie Versfeld and Evelyn Terblanche; and Manon Botha provides the cut flowers and potted plants in unusual vessels. At breakfast, the 'muddled' eggs – soft-boiled and mashed with aioli – are popular, as are pancakes and porridge, and at lunch, foraged greens feature in salads often tossed in their aunt's dressing. The bar showcases artisan spirits in subtly spiced cocktails. Closed Sundays. *176 Bree Street, T 021 823 8695, www.betweenus.capetown*

09.00 Sea Point Pavilion

The promenade that stretches from Green Point Lighthouse to the iconic Sea Point Pavilion (open 7am to 7pm in the summer) passes through three Atlantic suburbs; a highlight is the 1955 HQ of broadcaster SABC (209 St James Road), designed by architects Meiring & Naudé. The pavilion was built in the 1950s and has remained blissfully unchanged since then, despite often being eyed with zeal by developers.

Little of the ocean that surrounds Cape Town is swim-friendly — the Atlantic is far too cold and the Indian is a tiresome drive away — hence the popularity of the four saltwater pools found here, one of which is Olympic-sized. An alternative is Newlands Swimming Pool (T 021 671 2729), which is graced with a modernist stand topped by a floating swallow-tail-shaped canopy.
Beach Road, T 021 434 3341

10.30 South African National Gallery

Blockbuster shows by South Africans such as multimedia star William Kentridge and painter Marlene Dumas, and the continent's big names, including Ghanaian sculptor El Anatsui, have secured the SANG headline status. Opened in 1930, it's an architectural mishmash of Dutch colonial and Beaux Arts styles. Despite being neglected by the state, its patrons ensure that contemporary art remains high on the agenda, for instance by providing the capital to acquire Mary Sibande's 2010 *The Reign*, which depicts a black domestic worker astride a rearing horse. The extensive collection features Jane Alexander's *Butcher Boys*, from 1986, paintings by Peter Clarke, and pieces by expressionist Irma Stern. Textiles, drawings and photography are regularly shown too. *Government Avenue, Company's Garden, T 021 481 3970, www.iziko.org.za*

24 HOURS

11.30 Zeitz MOCAA
Thomas Heatherwick repurposed a 1920s grain warehouse, once Cape Town's tallest building, for this 2017 museum and hotel, but his key design gesture is found inside. Carved into the original cylindrical silos is a cathedral-esque atrium shaped like a corn kernel supported on concrete buttresses visible from the spiral stairs. In 100 (often rather pokey) halls, MOCAA displays 21st-century art from Africa and its diaspora, including pieces by South Africans such as visual activist Zanele Muholi, sculptor Mary Sibande and Capetonian Jody Paulsen, who creates vivid felt collages. Plonked on top is The Silo hotel (see p016), with interiors by Liz Biden that contrast dramatically with the stripped-down industrial vibe. Check it out over a tipple at The Willaston Bar.
S Arm Road, T 087 350 4777,
www.zeitzmocaa.museum

12.45 The Kitchen
Karen Dudley's eaterie is an institution. The Kitchen launched in 2009, coinciding with the emergence of a bustling arts hub along Sir Lowry Road (see p065). Decorated with antique crockery and kitchen oddities, its boho decor and made-with-love culinary ethos attract a diverse crowd of ad execs, hipsters and wealthy ladies with little dogs from the nicer suburbs. Bedrocks of the lunch menu are the legendary gourmet sandwiches, including the honey mustard sausage on an artisanal roll, and the salad platters – mix and match from 20 or so dishes like preserved lemon and courgette tabbouleh, and bulgar wheat with apple, hazelnut and raisin. If you're short on time, order to take away for a picnic at the Taal Monument (overleaf). Closed weekends.
111-113 Sir Lowry Road, T 021 462 2201, www.lovethekitchen.co.za

14.15 Taal Monument
Architect Jan van Wijk's remarkable 1975 tribute to Afrikaans, South Africa's unique hybrid language, is, if nothing else, a top picnic spot on the way to the winelands of Franschhoek and Stellenbosch (overleaf). Afrikaans is the third most widely spoken of the country's 11 official languages, after Zulu and Xhosa, and is a mixture of Dutch (mainly), French, English, German, Malay and indigenous languages – all of which are symbolically recognised in these huge granite columns. When this monument was built, Afrikaans was heavily associated with apartheid; the government policy of deeming it to be the compulsory language of instruction in schools led to the Soweto uprising of 1976. In Cape Town, 92 people were killed in the aftermath. Yet Afrikaans is still vibrant today and is the lingua franca beyond most of metropolitan South Africa.
Gabbema Doordrift Street, Paarl Mountain, T 021 863 4809, www.taalmuseum.co.za

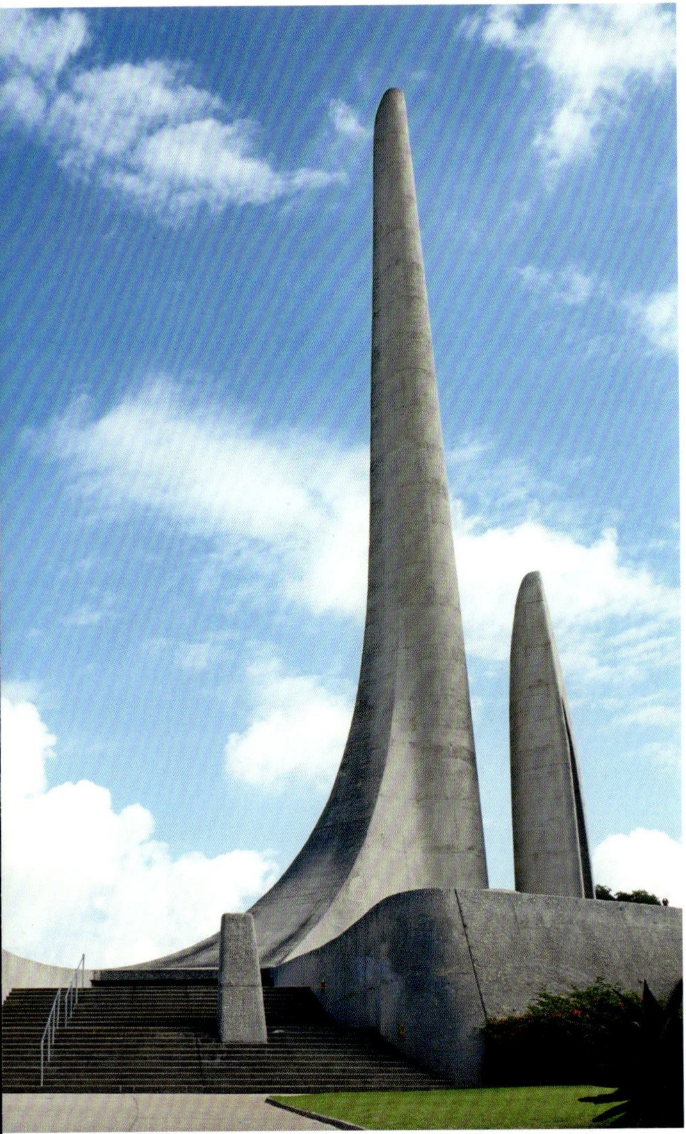

15.30 Delaire Graff Estate

Owned by billionaire diamond and gem dealer Laurence Graff, this stylish winery reopened in 2009 following a rebuild by architect Derick Henstra, whose previous projects include Mandela Rhodes Place in Cape Town. Situated on a rise facing the Simonsberg and Drakenstein mountains, the main building is bisected by a stone spine wall that runs the length of the site, parallel to a row of pin oak trees outside.

There is a tasting lounge (above) and two restaurants: an eponymous upscale bistro with marble fireplaces, and Asian-themed Indochine. London design firm David Collins oversaw the tasteful interiors throughout. The estate produces some outstanding whites, notably the Banghoek chardonnay, which has vanilla and honeycomb notes.
*R310, Helshoogte Pass, Stellenbosch,
T 021 885 8160, www.delaire.co.za*

18.00 The Twelve Apostles Spa

This property, which is perched stunningly above the Atlantic Ocean between Camps Bay and Llandudno, was once the source of controversy. In 1992, an advertising exec sold his isolated residence to a developer, who planned to transform it into a hotel. The locals were outraged and some models even staged a topless protest (a PR stunt for Cape Town's embryonic agencies), but councillors turned a blind eye. Any partial nudity now linked to The Twelve Apostles Hotel is confined to its spa. A 2012 redesign by Toni Tollman mixes Eastern ideals with marine-inspired murals; its best attribute is the sea vista from the two mountain gazebos. Full facilities include a saltwater flotation pool, ideal for managing jet lag, and an Arabic rasul cleansing chamber.
Victoria Road, T 021 437 9060, www.12apostleshotel.com

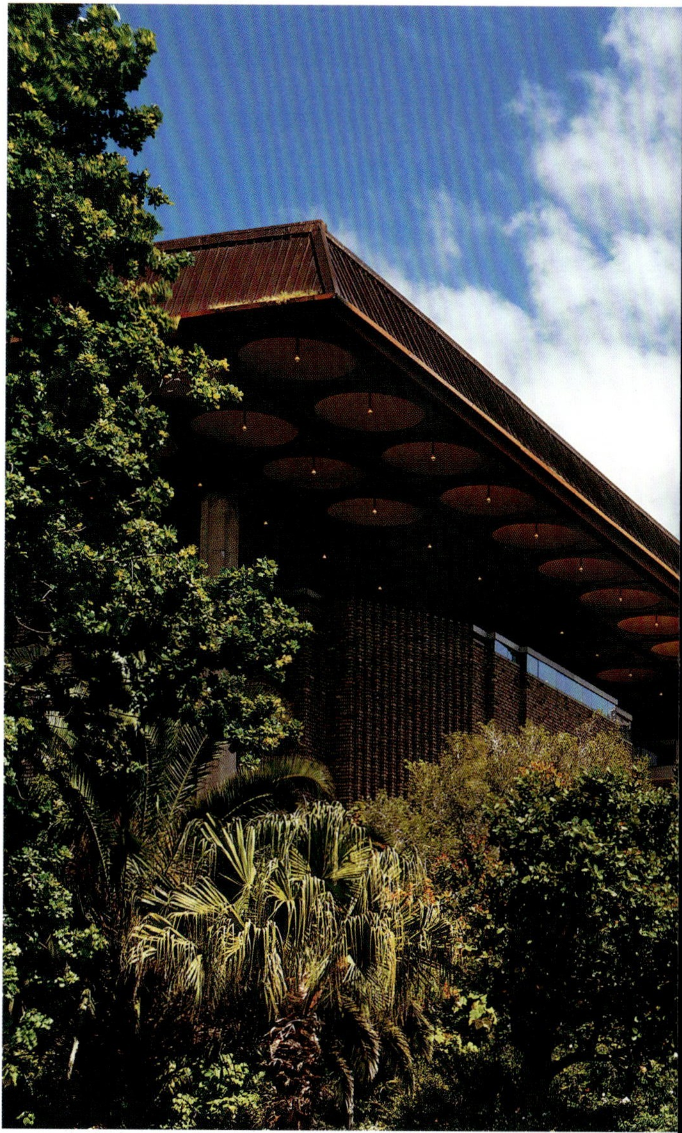

19.45 Baxter Theatre Centre
Among the city's notable theatres are The Fugard (T 021 461 4554) and this 1977 brick masterpiece by Jack Barnett. Also comprising a concert hall, it was open to all throughout segregation and continues to programme innovative community productions. The imposing exterior has intricate touches, such as the recessed orange dome lights.
Main Road, Rondebosch, T 021 685 7880

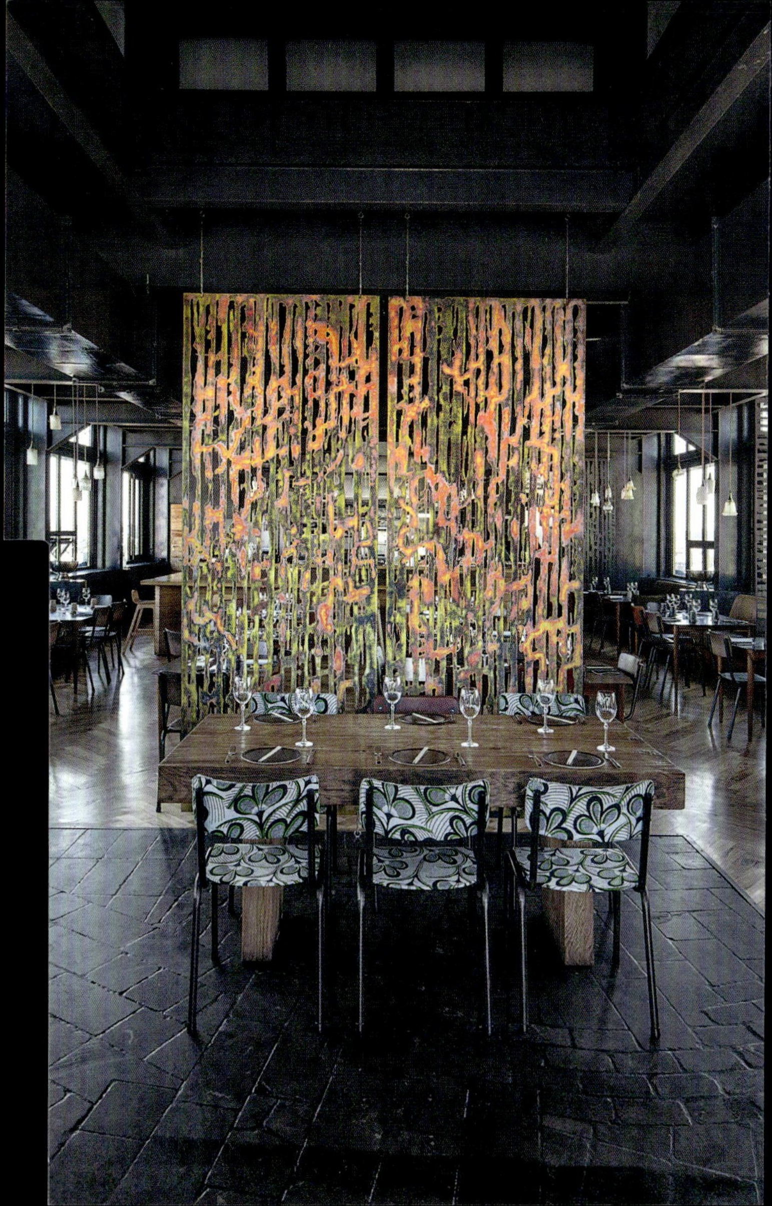

21.00 The Pot Luck Club

This hip restaurant on top of a disused silo ticks all the boxes, including terrific views of Cape Town's mixed-up urban fabric. An external lift exits onto a bridge, decorated with a bronze plate sporting a wild boar (the venue's logo) made by Otto du Plessis, and cobblestones by sculptor Egon Tania. Interiors feature wood accents, such as stone pine seating at diner-style counters, and herringbone parquetry. Chef Luke Dale-Roberts' (see p050) small-plate menu is split into the five tastes – for instance, doenjang-glazed tuna and kimchi (salty) or pork belly with smoked pecan butter and ash-baked celeriac (umami). The bar is functional; for late-night libations, we recommend Van Hunks (T 021 422 5422) or the roof at Tjing Tjing (T 021 422 4920). *The Old Biscuit Mill, 373-375 Albert Road, T 021 447 0804, www.thepotluckclub.co.za*

URBAN LIFE
CAFÉS, RESTAURANTS, BARS AND NIGHTCLUBS

In 2006 two regional establishments were, for the first time, listed among the world's best places to eat. La Colombe (Silvermist Wine Estate, Main Road, T 021 794 2390) has continued to impress, while accolades for The Test Kitchen (see p050) and Wolfgat (see p101) have entrenched the area's cachet as a foodie paradise. Although prices and service can raise eyebrows, and beachside eateries may get sloppy in high season, City Bowl spots such as Hemelhuijs (see p046) and Carne SA (see p052) are dependable, and restaurants in outer suburbs are often a revelation, in particular Harbour House (see p058) and Olympia Café (134 Main Road, T 021 788 6396), both in Kalk Bay. Many of the wineries have great dining options (see p034), and the hinterlands are dotted with standalone gems like Reuben's (2 Daniel Hugo Street, T 021 876 3772) in Franschhoek.

The turnover here tends to be high; venues can be the in-thing for six months and then promptly fall off the radar at the end of 'season' – the busy summer period between November and March. However, you can't go wrong with institutions like La Perla (209 Beach Road, T 021 439 9538), with its perennially popular terrace, and Societi Bistro (50 Orange Street, T 021 424 2100), set in an 1813 Georgian home with garden seating. The Hussar Grill (108 Camps Bay Drive, T 021 438 0151) steakhouse predates the culinary renaissance; its survival alone is enough of a testimony.
For full addresses, see Resources.

Mulberry & Prince

Emerging chefs Cornel Mostert, a local, and Brooklynite Cynthia Rivera met at culinary school in New York, and here cook modern American cuisine in a venue named after a favourite street corner. Cape Town firm Atelier Interiors devised a gallery-esque setting, with a dusty-pink entrance (a hue echoed throughout), a slate-clad bar and exposed stone; stained glass and copper elements by Conrad Van der Westhuizen; Pedersen + Lennard tables; and abstract paintings by Kurt Pio. There's a menu of inventive sharing plates such as bacalhau fritters, scarlet kale and foraged pine ring mushroom 'carbonara', salt-baked seabass, and panna cotta with liquorice caramel. It is open 7pm to 10pm from Wednesday to Saturday, and for a sugary Sunday brunch. *12 Pepper Street, T 021 422 3301, www.mulberryandprince.co.za*

La Tête

Located in the rapidly developing financial district in a restored 1930s art deco corner building, La Tête serves what some locals still consider to be hoi polloi fare. Its ethos was inspired by the nose-to-tail philosophy of Fergus Henderson's St John in London, where chef Giles Edwards, who founded this restaurant with his brother James in 2016, spent five years. That mentorship is clear: as well as brilliantly executed cheap cuts, including devilled chicken hearts, ox tongue, brains on toast, baked pig's head and flattened ear, the menu lists hake and chips, roast quail, and mussels with leek and bacon. The wine selection is excellent, particularly the reds by AA Badenhorst and Thelema. The perforated white squares on the walls are not art but sound absorbers.
17 Bree Street, T 021 418 1299,
www.latete.co.za

The Moveable Feast
The junction of Buitengracht Street and Kloof Nek Road used to be a backpackers' hangout until the arrival of refined Kyoto Garden (T 021 422 2001), which serves an exquisite tasting menu in a Zen setting, and genial haunt The Power & The Glory (T 021 422 2108), where the pretzel hotdogs have proved a big hit. Opened upstairs from the latter in 2018, this French-inspired bistro is owned by Parisians Vincent John Soimaud and Rafael Wallon, who have decked it out with Thonet 'No 14' chairs, marble-top tables and faceted mirrors. The steak with béarnaise and frites is legendary, although the pan-fried butter-and-thyme sea bass is a fine alternative. The neon-lit bar serves craft beers and cocktails to a bohemian crowd drawn by the frequent drag shows.
13 Kloof Nek Road, T 087 897 9749, www.themoveablefeast.co.za

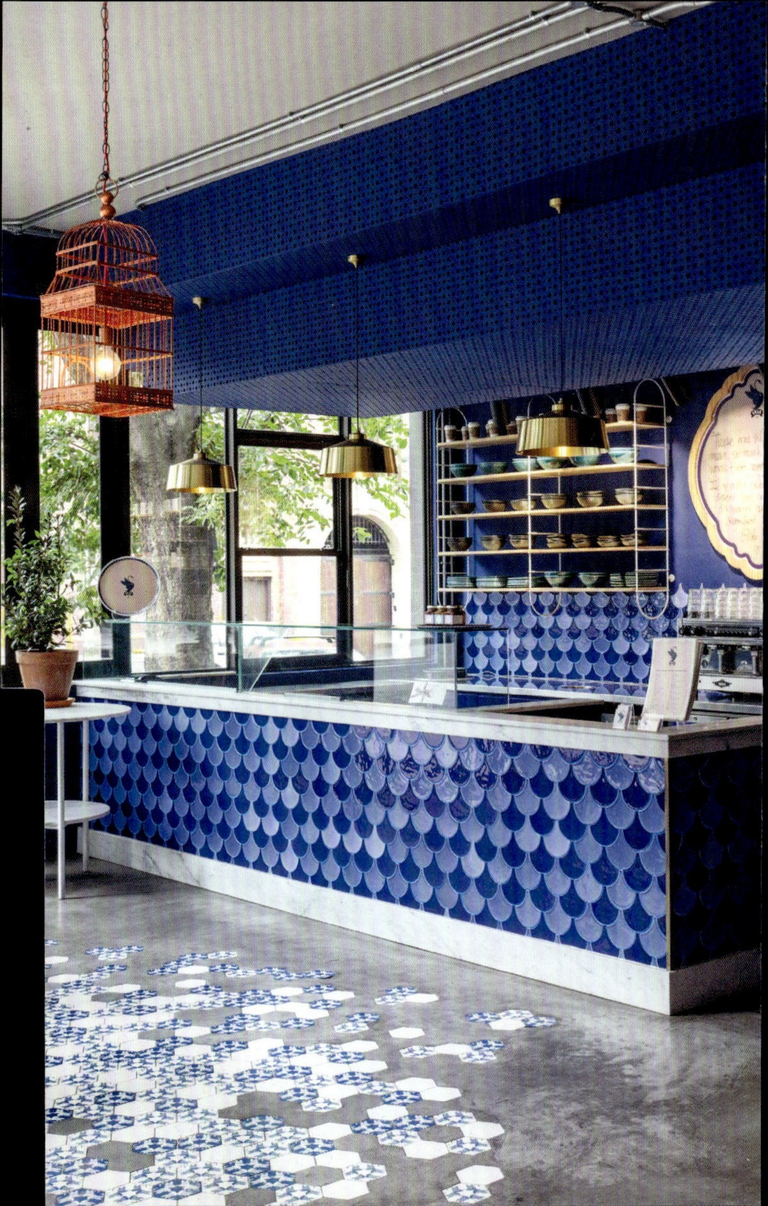

Swan Café

French-born Jessica Rushmere's East City crêperie is immensely popular with a hip local crowd, in part for its feminine decor, overseen by furniture designer Haldane Martin. Blue shades dominate, including in the large reproductions of swan-theme works by Leonardo da Vinci and Jean-Léon Gérôme. Parisian café culture is evoked in the tiled bar counter with scallop motif, marble tables with coloured iron bases, lights hung in copper birdcages and staff dressed in Breton stripes. The sweetest option is the salted caramel with Ferrero Rocher and Nutella (you may wish to order one of the impressive salads to balance matters out); we could not resist a galette filled with blue cheese, red wine-poached pears, prosciutto and candied walnuts.
*Buitenkant Street/Barrack Street,
T 079 454 4758, www.swancafe.co.za*

Hemelhuijs

The attractive sans-serif signage outside proprietor Jacques Erasmus' central city bistro, launched in 2010, hints at what one can expect inside – simple, unembellished luxury. The trim modern furnishings were custom-made, nicely complementing the sleek shelving, which is used to showcase Hemelhuijs' Asian-inspired homewares: the 'Sepia' table range is particularly striking, as well as functional, as it can retain heat for up to half an hour. While the underlying philosophy is *wabi sabi*, it's offset by some decadent arrangements of fresh flowers and objets trouvés. The seasonal menu has a number of classic staples, including the *frikkadel* (South African meatballs), which are served here with a buttery mash. Wash it all down with the house sauvignon blanc.
71 Waterkant Street, T 021 418 2042,
www.hemelhuijs.co.za

Grand Africa Café & Beach

It's quite amazing what a few truckloads of imported sand can do. Situated on a small harbour beside the V&A Waterfront, this café and restaurant located on an artificial beach adopts a bohemian baroque theme and runs with it. The dining hall is set in an old boathouse decorated with chandeliers and bistro chairs, whereas outside, choose between terrace seating under parasols or loafing about on loungers. There's plenty of seafood on offer, as well as pizza and Med classics, but cocktails are the main draw; try the watermelon martini. The Grand is a lifestyle pitch, hence the retail boutique, which sells deluxe candles and swimwear. A roster of international DJs takes to the decks at weekends, and it gets congested at sundown in particular, so book ahead.
1 Haul Road, T 071 382 7044,
www.grandafrica.com

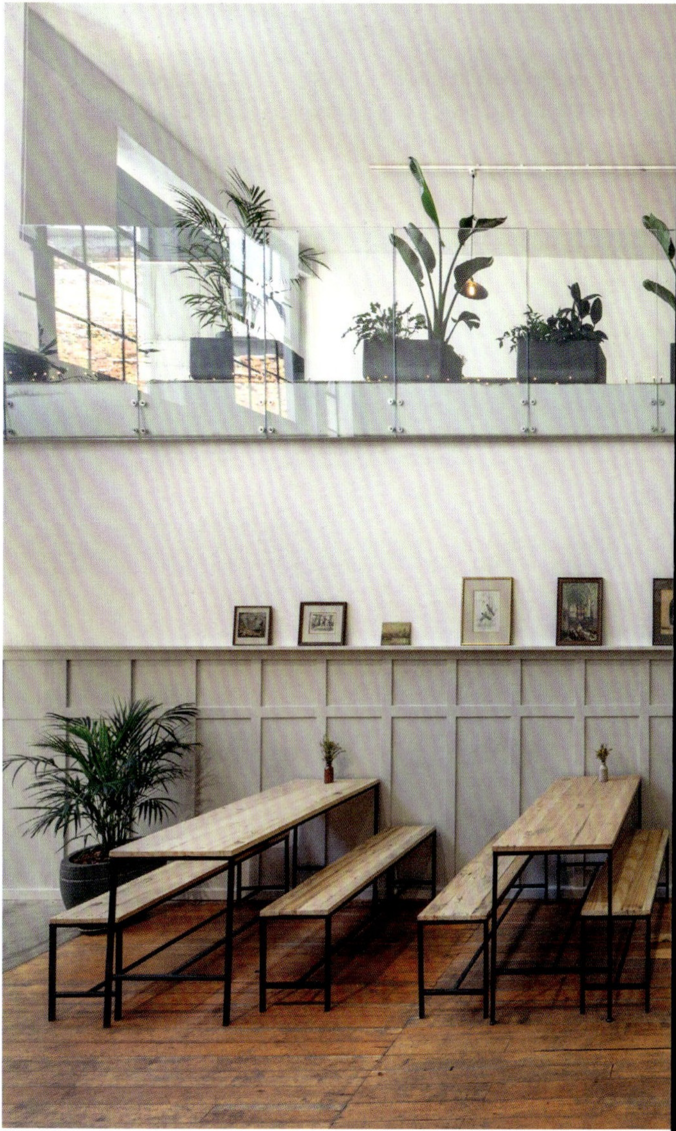

The Gin Bar
Established in a cupboard-sized venue fronting onto a courtyard, in 2018 this popular speakeasy took over a defunct gallery in the same building. Now spread over two levels, with separate bars, it serves five medicinal-themed cocktails, said to alleviate all manner of ailments; there are also 130 varieties of craft gin.
64a Wale Street, T 071 241 2277
www.theginbar.co.za

The Test Kitchen

Brit chef Luke Dale-Roberts moved to Cape Town in 2006 and built his reputation at La Colombe (see p040), launching TKK four years later to diversify. A 2017 overhaul by his furniture-designer wife Sandalene and architect Maurice Paliaga created a pair of distinct spaces to experience his 21-plate globe-trotting tasting menu, served to 40 people nightly. The Dark Room, with leather seats and a burnt-wood mural by Hannelie Coetzee, is a loungey first stop to sample an array of starters like blesbok tartare. The Light Room (above) is a more conventional dining environment. Here, past creations have included smoked scallop sashimi with mushroom ponzu and Jerusalem artichoke, lobster bibimbap, and assiette of goat and lamb; there are also tea and wine pairings.
The Old Biscuit Mill, 373-375 Albert Road, T 021 447 2337, www.thetestkitchen.co.za

The Black Sheep

This smartly appointed bistro is situated at the upper, suburban end of Kloof Street and is still something of a local secret. Split across three levels, it has a street-facing bar with domed copper pendant lamps, two dining spaces, and a statement wall of wooden cast-offs that have been organised into a clever design feature. Previous to partnering with Chilean co-owner Jorge Silva, chef Jonathan Japha supervised the kitchen at Fork (T 021 424 6334), one of the first Cape Town eateries to serve Spanish 'pinchos'. Here, Japha's chalkboard menu changes almost daily – past dishes have included slow-roasted kudu loin, grilled venison with thick-cut chips, and seared tuna. The mezzanine lounge (above) is a discreet spot for post-prandial confabs.
104 Kloof Street, T 021 426 2661,
www.blacksheeprestaurant.co.za

Carne SA
When gregarious restaurateur Giorgio Nava opened 95 Keerom (T 021 422 0765), many were seduced by the pared-down excellence of his modern Italian cooking with a Milanese accent. South Africans, however, are avid red-meat eaters, a fact that encouraged Nava to unveil this 2008 split-level venue in the former Cape Law Chambers. Never mind the dark, masculine interior, it's the beef, lamb and venison cuts explained with consummate seriousness by well-drilled staff that truly define this eaterie. The house speciality is the 1.2kg La Fiorentina T-bone; the aged prime rib is highly recommended too. For more casual occasions, pop by the Kloof Street outpost (T 021 426 5566), where options include marbled spider steak and *picanha*.
70 Keerom Street, T 021 424 3460, www.carne-sa.com

URBAN LIFE

Greenhouse
The pitch is simple enough: fine dining in a tastefully decorated conservatory that is attached to The Cellars-Hohenort hotel, a lovely property set away from the bustle on the forested slopes of Table Mountain. Proving himself equal to this Eden, chef Farrel Hirsch has devised an expeditionary tasting menu encompassing flavours from across the region. Highlights include the caramel-smoked duck with truffled liver mousse and hibiscus beets, and game fish, quinoa, seaweed and grapefruit served with blue prawn steamed tableside on a hot stone. The 45-seater venue comprises three salons (glasshouse, above) and local firm Hotcocoa's refined interior scheme is accented by blond ashwood and oyster-hued leather furnishings. Book ahead.
93 Brommersvlei Road, T 021 795 6226,
www.greenhouserestaurant.co.za

Clarke's Bar & Dining Room

In 2011, Lyndall Maunder left Superette (see p061), where she was the head chef, and opened Clarke's, a no-frills update on the diner. A smooth metal counter and simple pendant lighting underscore the venue's utilitarian approach to decor (and menu design), although the surroundings are warmed by a collection of terracotta-potted greenery. In summer, the front pine deck is an ideal position for people-watching. Clarke's legendary 210g grass-fed beef burger certainly ranks among the best in the city, loaded with Underberg cheese in a house-baked bun, and served with fries. The bistro-style dishes include a hot dog topped with kimchi and Sriracha hot sauce. Local craft beers, such as Jack Black's and Birkenhead, are offered on tap.
133 Bree Street, T 087 470 0165,
www.clarkesdining.co.za

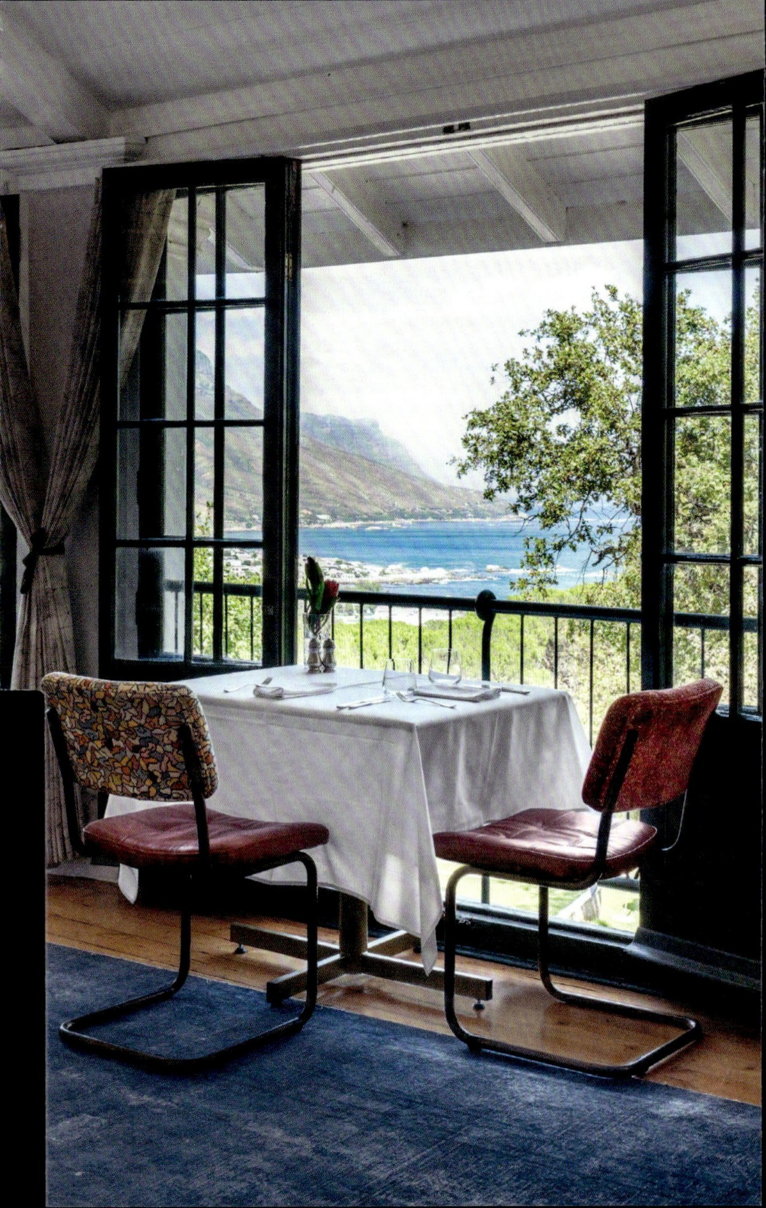

Salsify at The Roundhouse

Luke Dale-Roberts' (see p050) Camps Bay venture, launched in 2018, occupies a 1786 mountain hideaway, formerly Lord Charles Somerset's hunting lodge. Sandalene Dale-Roberts took care of the renovation and installed graffiti murals in the lounge by Louis de Villiers, a Horus-like sculpture at the entrance by Otto du Plessis of Bronze Age (see p064) and Persian rugs and retro steel-frame chairs in the airy dining room. The à la carte lists South African favourites including charred beef fillet with truffled pepper sauce, but it is the seven-course tasting menu devised with resident chef Ryan Cole that is the real draw, featuring delights such as quail breast with Scotch egg, sticky tomato lamb rib, and roasted line fish. Reserve a month in advance.
*1 Roundhouse Road, off Kloof Road,
T 021 010 6444, www.salsify.co.za*

Harbour House

This glass-box seafood restaurant would be a tourist trap anywhere else, but here, built on a breakwater in Kalk Bay, it works as a modest temple to simply prepared fish. The style is North Atlantic with Mediterranean influences and much of the day's catch is from the boats docked in the little harbour. Feast on sautéed calamari with smoked paprika, grilled crayfish, and kingklip, a cusk eel that is a popular local delicacy. The floor-to-ceiling windows face out over False Bay and, if you're lucky, from July to November, you might spot southern right whales as they come inshore to calf. If you are unable to secure a table (weekends are prime time), laidback Tiger's Milk (T 021 286 6805) downstairs has an evergreen menu and serves impressive cocktails.
1st floor, Kalk Bay Harbour, T 021 788 4136, www.harbourhouse.co.za

The Haas Collective

After a stint in Bo-Kaap, where it gained a following for its single-origin coffees and covetable design objects, Haas moved into this Edwardian property done out with a boho medley of retro and upcycled chairs and tables, and a taxidermied antelope. The beautiful, unusual items dotted about are for sale, from jewellery by Ashleigh McCulloch to paintings by Vanessa Berlein, sculptures by Grainne McHugh, and Rene Wentzel's ceramic skulls, all of which add to the gothic vibe. At breakfast, fuel up on pastries, toast and eggs, or come at lunch for seared tuna with tabbouleh, or bunny chow (chicken curry presented in a hollow loaf), a version of the Durban street snack. Haas' popularity, however, still rests on its java. Open until 5pm (3pm at weekends). *19 Buitenkant Street, T 021 461 1812, www.haascollective.com*

El Burro Taqueria
This is a single-plate offshoot of the buzzy Green Point Mexican eaterie El Burro (T 021 433 2364) and its sister bar downstairs, the lovely tile-and-wood Cabrito, which serves tequila and craft beers. The taqueria has a congenial, laidback vibe and ups the hip factor of a buzzy Tamboerskloof enclave (see p043). The eye-popping interiors are a visual fiesta of bright, happy colours, as steel-and-wood stools in sky-blue, mauve and yellow cluster around canteen tables. There are tacos filled with Baja-style fish-of-the-day with avocado and smoked jalapeño, and *chilorio* pork with chilli and garlic, as well as quesadillas, and it also specialises in ceviche. It's co-owned by the Berolsky brothers, whose other enterprises include three-storey burger joint and bar Royale Eatery (T 021 422 4536) in the CBD.
12-16 Kloof Nek Road, T 021 433 3554

Superette

Due to its expansive windows and splashes of canary yellow, this light and breezy café is hard to miss at The Woodstock Exchange entrance. It was launched by local Cameron Munro and New Yorker Justin Rhodes, the duo behind Whatiftheworld gallery (see p067) and Neighbourgoods Market (see p088). The fibreboard benches and 'Dual-Purpose' wood shelving, which displays a selection of deli items, including Deluxe Coffeeworks beans and Prince Albert olive oils, are by Xandre Kriel (see p068). But it is Munro's no-fuss menu that attracts the area's tech employees, artists, hipsters and, on Saturday mornings, suburbanites. Order soft-boiled eggs served with soldiers and lemon-dressed greens, or a pork belly sandwich with honey-roasted apple sauce. *66 Albert Road, T 021 802 5525, www.superette.co.za*

INSIDER'S GUIDE
MARSI VAN DE HEUVEL, ARTIST

'The best thing about Cape Town is living between the mountain and the sea,' says artist Marsi van de Heuvel, who resides in the City Bowl Suburbs and is represented by Smith (see p078). Yet she adds South Africa's oldest city still has the energy of a teenager: 'It is excitable, gifted with lots of potential, but still experiencing growing pains.'

On days off, she has a standing order for crispy eggs on sourdough at Clarke's (see p055), 'and their Bloody Mary is the best in town'. A fan of the city's independent boutiques, she makes a beeline to Margot Molyneux (69 Roeland Street, T 021 461 4565) for classic-cut dresses, AKJP Studio (see p089) for more than 20 labels, and mini department store Sans (277 Main Road, T 021 205 4555): 'Yaniv Chen's Japanese-style interior is the icing on the cake.' For lunch she might pop by Between Us (see p026), or pick up picnic items at the Tardis-like Olive Branch Deli (50 Kloof Street, T 073 847 5499).

In the evening, Van de Heuvel recommends the terrace at The Dark Horse (145 Kloof Street, T 021 422 0825) for a sundowner, and dining on springbok across the road at The Black Sheep (see p051). Alternatively, retro The Athletic Club & Social (35 Buitengracht Street, T 021 012 5331) serves tapas and drinks over three 'intimate' floors, and The Moveable Feast (see p043) has 'quality music and a vibrant bar'. For an uninhibited boogie, she heads to LGBT-friendly Zero21 Social Club (46 Canterbury Street, T 071 760 3178).

For full addresses, see Resources.

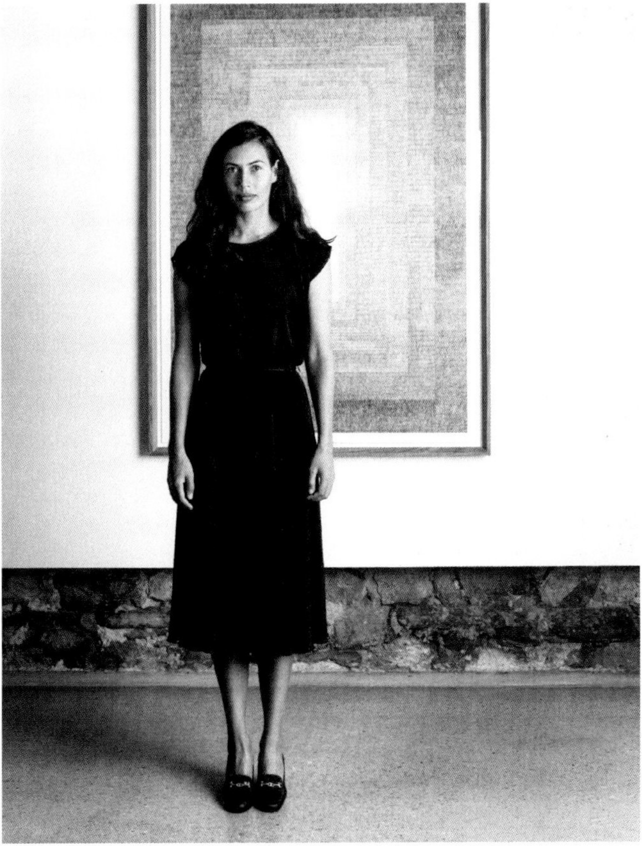

ART AND DESIGN
GALLERIES, STUDIOS AND PUBLIC SPACES

Cape Town's design scene is steeped in settler tradition; carpenters and silversmiths have been making fine furnishings since the 17th century, and Dutch, French and English influences still dominate. Indeed, signs of its African-ness might seem elusive. Guga S'Thebe (see p076) provides a window into a consciously local style, but the essence of the city's artisanal character lies in a mix-and-match attitude and seat-of-the-pants improvisation, seen at hubs such as The Woodstock Exchange (66-68 Albert Road, T 021 486 5999) and Mason's Press (7 Ravenscraig Road, T 021 424 1210). The pinnacle of creativity is reached in the refined pieces by Atang Tshikare (see p071) and Bronze Age (1b Coode Crescent, T 021 421 2223), and the divergent talents represented by Southern Guild (see p068).

The 2018 launch of the Norval Foundation (see p072) capped an impressive 15 months in which a slew of private initiatives, from Zeitz MOCAA (see p030) to A4 Arts (see p079) and the Maitland Institute (372 Voortrekker Road), a not-for-profit upstart in an old meat-processing factory, arrived to cement Cape Town's reputation as an emerging art destination. Commercial galleries championing African talent, such as Momo (16 Buiten Street, T 021 424 5140) and SMAC (145 Sir Lowry Road, T 021 461 1029), are clustered in the CBD and Woodstock, an area that's emblazoned with murals by the likes of Faith XLVII (see p074), Andrzej Urbanski and DALeast.
For full addresses, see Resources.

Stevenson

Sir Lowry Road, which slices right through Woodstock, is home to two of the country's leading contemporary galleries— this one and Goodman (T 021 462 7573), which pioneered the art market in South Africa. Both of them inhabit cleverly conceived spaces. Stevenson, which has been blazing a trail since back in 2003, is now almost museum-like in ambition, often featuring quirky interventions by young artists on its entrance ramp. It's markedly strong on photography — it represents Pieter Hugo, Guy Tillim, Zanele Muholi and Viviane Sassen — and painting, having exhibited the acclaimed Odili Donald Odita, Zander Blom and Penny Siopis. Another draw is Burundian sculptor Serge Alain Nitegeka, who took part in 'Schema' (above).
Buchanan Building, 160 Sir Lowry Road, T 021 462 1500, www.stevenson.info

Open House
This 10.5m painted-steel sculpture was commissioned by the local government in order to celebrate 20 years of democracy. Also affirming the 'Live Design, Transform Life' mantra of the city's 2014 tenure as World Design Capital, Jacques Coetzer's creation quotes the geometry of the area's ubiquitous two-storey Victorian buildings (see p070), and the simple construction materials, such as corrugated iron, that are used in poor communities. Essentially a freestanding frontage, it is universally accessible; its 'Open' sign reinforces that message. It is located next to Hannes van der Merwe's 1974 modernist tower, whose facade was spruced up with a white beam lattice in an update of the whole ensemble by local practice Jakupa. However, Coetzer's thought piece is the most visible statement.
Long Street/Dorp Street

Whatiftheworld

Founded in the early noughties by Cameron Munro and Justin Rhodes in East City, this gallery forged its reputation in Woodstock where it occupied a restored synagogue. In 2018, another move to the city centre saw a scaling down in size only, as it continues to represent names such as photographers Athi-Patra Ruga and Mohau Modisakeng, and retains its brattish, hipster roots, often showcasing sparky young artists. Thania Petersen, whose heritage is Cape Malay, incorporated prayer mats, photography, video and installation in 'IQRA' (*In Defence of Our Memories*, above), a salvo against Islamic fundamentalism. Also on the books are painters Mia Chaplin and Ruby Swinney, and Lungiswa Gqunta, whose works have featured barbed wire and broken bottles.
16 Buiten Street, T 021 422 1066, www.whatiftheworld.com

068

ART/DESIGN

Southern Guild
Run by husband and wife Julian and Trevyn McGowan, Southern Guild shows high-end local and national design as if it were art. It moved from its Woodstock warehouse in 2017, joining Zeitz MOCAA (see p030) and Daor Contemporary (T 021 001 2633) in the emerging Silo District. Devised by VDMMA and Jacobs Parker, the venue comprises a gallery for solo exhibitions and a furniture showroom (left) that displays its in-house line and tie-ups like a Wiid Design bench given a Lionel Smit paint job (foreground). Other stars of the roster include Andile Dyalvane (see p094), Xandre Kriel, Porky Hefer, known for his distinctive conceptual nature- and bird-inspired pieces ('Behd', rear left, and 'M Heloise', rear right), and Chuma Maweni, whose carved ebonised timber and glazed clay 'Imbizo' collection (table, centre) features precise patterns.
Shop 5b, Silo 5, T 021 461 2856, www.southernguild.co.za

Ebony/Curated
Founded by Dewald Prinsloo, Leonard de Villiers and Brit photographer Marc Stanes in 2007 as a showcase for pan-African art and design, Ebony opened this city centre outlet four years later in a typical Victorian property – restored but unembellished. It has a reputation for spotlighting emerging talent, such as Patrick Bongoy, from Congo, who is known for his enigmatic sculptures and tapestries made from woven fragments of car-tyre inner tubes, and the powerful embroideries of Kimathi Mafafo, from the Northern Cape. Travel to the Franschhoek HQ (T 021 876 4477) for Capetonian John Newdigate's painted porcelain vessels and the in-house furniture line of midcentury modern-style pieces produced locally from fine woods and fabrics like animal hide.
67 Loop Street, T 021 424 9985, www.ebonycurated.com

ART/DESIGN

Atang Tshikare

Bloemfontein-born furniture designer Atang Tshikare moved to the Mother City in 2009. His Tswana heritage is evident in works that explore Afrofuturism through their arresting patterns, strange shapes, earthy palettes and assorted textures. For the irresistibly tactile 'Kae-Kapa-Kae' (above) and 'Yang-Kapa-Yang', a pair of bronze stools, he was inspired by the rocky outcrops and mythology of Modimolle, a butte in Limpopo, creating the surface indentations with his fingers. He worked with local studio Casamento on the 'Leifo' chair, which features charred-effect wood, woven grass and brass beads. Okha (T 021 461 7233) carries his spindly 'Kaggen' side table, a homage to the trickster folk god Mantis, while other conceptual pieces are shown at Southern Guild (see p068).
www.atangtshikare.com

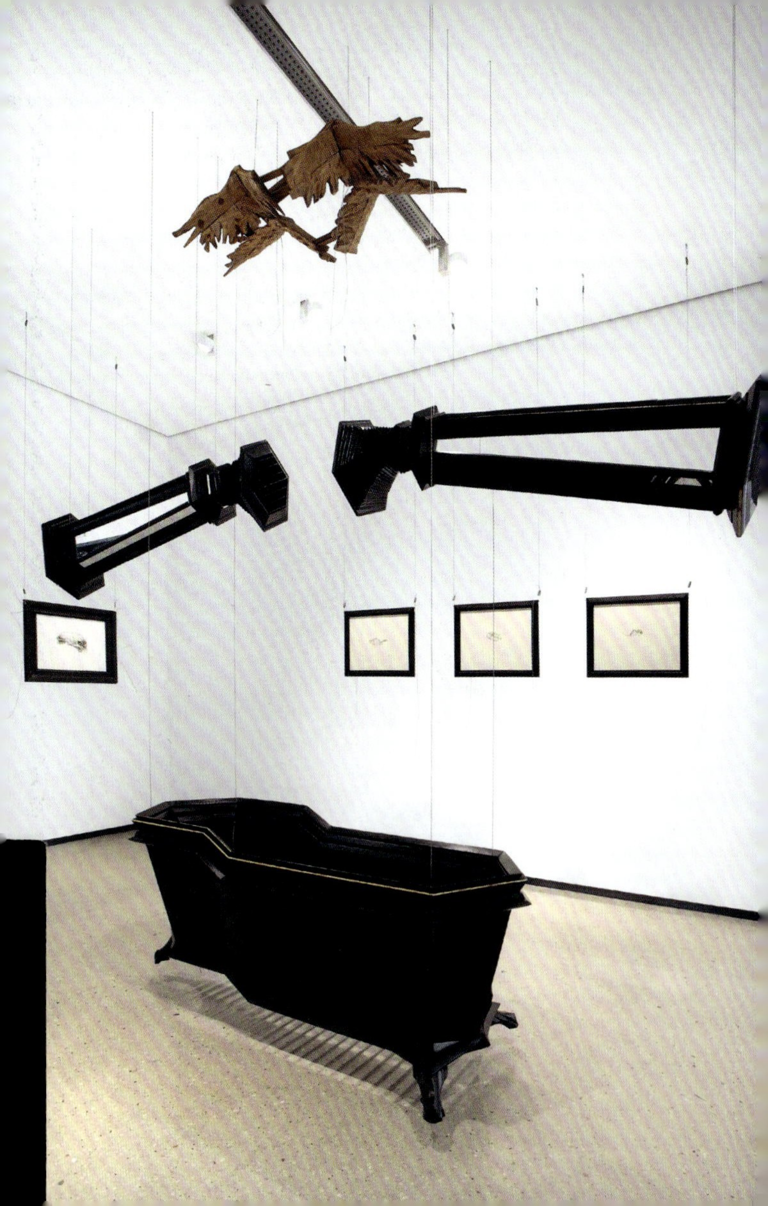

Norval Foundation

The Norval family's not-for-profit museum, located in Tokai, just south of Constantia, is giving Zeitz MOCAA (see p030) a serious run for its money. Architects DHK devised a grand pavilion with off-shutter concrete walls, a cantilevering roof and a soaring glass frontage that frames the surrounding wetlands, vineyards and sculpture garden. The nine halls, spread over two floors, are voluminous. Rotating shows often feature South Africans, including photographer David Goldblatt, sculptor Sydney Kumalo and Cape Town-based Wim Botha, whose 'Heliostat' retrospective (*Vanitas Toilette*, opposite) explored refraction. Or you might discover art from across the continent, like installations by Ghanaian Ibrahim Mahama and textiles by Malian Abdoulaye Konaté. *4 Steenberg Road, T 087 654 5900, www.norvalfoundation.org*

Faith XLVII

Street artist Faith XLVII blew up in the early 2000s with a series of murals, many with a political message. One of the most poignant appeared in 2010 at a boatyard near The Woodstock Exchange and portrayed an angel weeping over a grave identified as South Africa's Freedom Charter. It also offered sharp comment on the district's gentrification amidst a citywide housing crisis. This 2014 work is one of two large murals of statuesque women appearing on a government housing block flanking Philip Kgosana Drive. Entitled 'Harvest' and embedded with LEDs, it was created as part of a crowdfunding project to install street lighting in a squatter settlement in Khayelitsha. Faith XLVII's pop-figurative style is available to own in smaller format at Everard Read/CIRCA (T 021 418 4527).
59 Philip Kgosana Drive, Zonnebloem

Blank Projects

Founded as a not-for-profit in Bo-Kaap by sculptor Jonathan Garnham, Blank Projects championed tricksy artists throughout the noughties. Things changed after a 2010 relocation to Woodstock and a newfound commercial focus, although it retained its spirit with feisty shows, such as those by Igshaan Adams, whose installations often explore mixed-race culture, using materials including tapestries and discarded objects. Locals Cinga Samson and Jared Ginsburg helped buoy the reputation before Blank moved again in 2017, into the old Southern Guild (see p068) space, with its lofty ceiling and elegant parquetry. Here, Bronwyn Katz presented steel-wool sculptures (*X*, above) beside audio and video in an experiential statement on a disappearing language.
10 Lewin Street, T 021 462 4276, www.blankprojects.com

Guga S'Thebe

Indigenous craft is poorly represented in Cape Town, an imbalance that this mixed-use cultural centre in Langa township aims to plug. There are six studios occupied by local artists, a 200-capacity theatre and a crafts shop; hand-painted ceramics stand out over the carved-wood curios. But the chief reason to visit is the building. Opened in 1999, it is one of more than 100 socially conscious projects designed and effectively enabled by Carin Smuts, who creates low-cost public structures in consultation with communities, and won the 2008 Global Award for Sustainable Architecture. Guga S'Thebe is covered in murals and mosaics and references a traditional settlement: its golden cone is a contemporary take on the circular hut. Drop by independently, or on a tour with Cape Capers (T 021 448 3117).
King Langalibalele Street, T 021 695 3493

ART/DESIGN

Smith

Pedestrianised Church Street is a hub of galleries and design boutiques, including the bellwether AVA (T 021 424 7436), which launched here in 1971. Candace Marshall-Smith's venture was a fine addition in 2015. Architects Reanne Urbain and Alex McGee made a feature of the original 250-year-old stonework in sections of exposed wall, and installed a courtyard to divide the space. Smith opened with an exhibition by local painter Kurt Pio called 'I Love Cape Town' (above) that incorporated surfboards as canvases. Particularly dynamic is its programme of female artists, among them Marsi van de Heuvel (see p062), painters Jeanne Gaigher and Claire Johnson, and Michaela Younge, whose narrative appliqué pieces blend craft with macabre themes.
56 Church Street, T 021 422 0814, www.smithstudio.co.za

A4 Arts Foundation

Shunning sales talk and gallery pretensions for an experimental model, incubated in an late-1800s coral-coloured warehouse, A4 is a fascinating East City addition. Set across three floors is an exhibition space, in which artists are given latitude to develop shows, a library that's used for anything from book launches to hackathons and modern dance, and a studio for residencies. Romanian Dan Perjovschi lived here for a couple of weeks to create 'The Black and White Cape Town Report' (above), which playfully mocked local mores in his trademark style. Other past presentations have featured Unathi Mkonto, whose works draw on fashion and architecture, and pieces from the collection of founder Wendy Fisher, a highlight being those by the pioneering Ernest Mancoba.
23 Buitenkant Street, T 010 880 2595, www.a4arts.org

ARCHITOUR
A GUIDE TO CAPE TOWN'S ICONIC BUILDINGS

Cape Town possesses few signature public buildings. The centre is littered with stolid colonial and apartheid-era offerings and bland corporate towers, but there are some highlights. Customs House (Heerengracht Street) is a robust example of 1960s SA modernism, and the 89m Naspers Centre (40 Heerengracht Street), from 1962, was given an aluminium skin evoking roots in 2015. Yet the urban milieu is as notable for projects that went awry. In Claremont, the Werdmuller Centre (Main Road), a brutalist masterpiece by Roelof Uytenbogaardt, was a daring achievement in 1975, but it is boarded up as battle rages over its future. Then there are the stunted flyovers. The plan to link the Atlantic suburbs to the Eastern Boulevard ran out of funds in 1977, resulting in roads that end abruptly in mid-air.

However, leisure is now slowly transforming the city. Two major museums, Zeitz MOCAA (see p012) and the Norval Foundation (see p072) show singular responses to its contrasting landscapes. The most lauded projects are social, from schools to police stations and Mokena Makeka's 2010 makeover of the 1950s central Railway Station (Adderley Street, T 080 065 6463). You'll see construction cranes from the City Bowl to Sea Point, but most new-builds are me-too condos or offices; Team Architects' 236 Buitengracht Street, an oxidised concrete-and-glass interloper among the Cape Dutch and Georgian terrace homes in Bo-Kaap, is a refreshing antidote.
For full addresses, see Resources.

Centenary Tree Canopy Walkway
Once owned by Cecil John Rhodes, the 528-hectare Eden on the eastern slopes of Table Mountain became Kirstenbosch National Botanical Garden in 1913, and has recently been shedding its fuddy-duddy reputation. The summer concert series is perennially popular, with acts ranging from the Cape Town Philharmonic Orchestra to The Pixies. Then there are the manmade interventions, notably contemporary sculpture by Dylan Lewis, and this 12m-high, crescent-shaped steel-and-timber sky bridge through the arboretum. Designed by Mark Thomas and Christopher Bisset, the 130m-long walkway is known as 'The Boomslang' (Tree Snake) and has been a huge hit. In fact, it is often congested, much like the road connecting the CBD to this temperate part of the city.
Rhodes Drive, Newlands, T 021 799 8800, www.sanbi.org/gardens/kirstenbosch

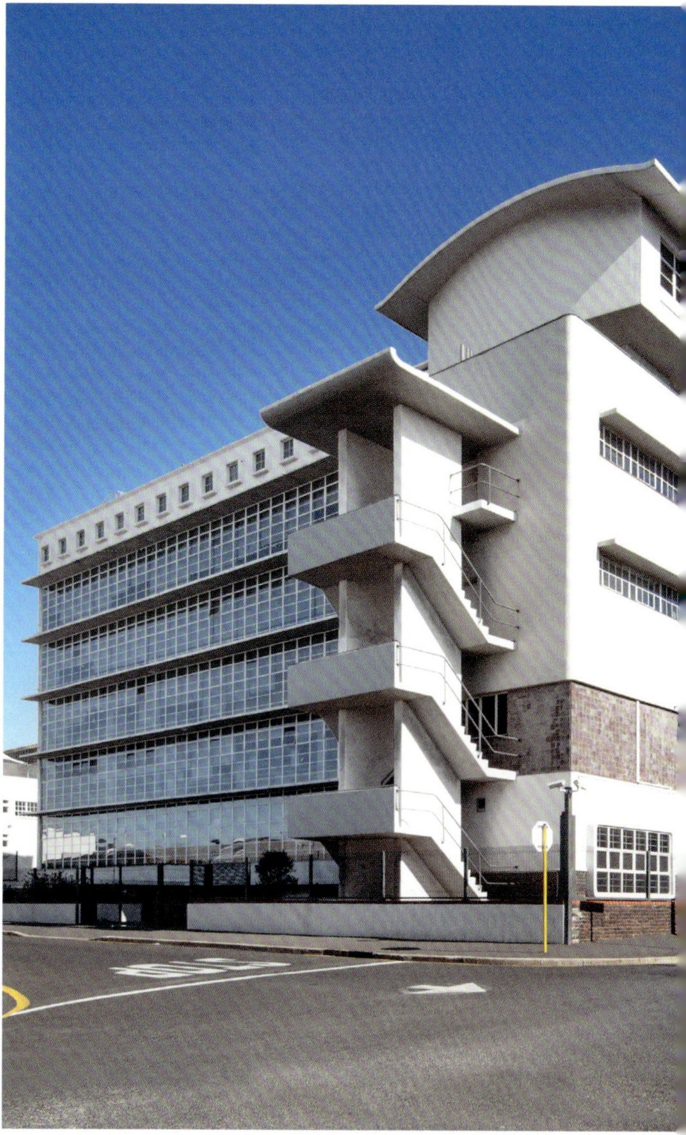

Rex Trueform
Along with the Silo District (see p068), and Mariendahl Brewery (T 021 658 7440) in Newlands, this iconic Salt River factory is a key part of Cape Town's industrial heritage. The original functionalist building by local architect Max Policansky opened in 1938, and is distinctive for its sawtooth roof and curved glass stairwell. The taller structure (left), a modernist ensemble by city firm Andrews and Niegeman, with wire-mesh windows along the Victoria Road facade and a wonderfully geometric fire escape, came a decade later. Rex Trueform once had its mens and womenswear stocked in Harrods, but it ceased manufacturing in 2005 – the complex is now an office park. Many original features remain, although not so easy to spot from the outside are the separate entrances and staff amenities that were introduced in 1948: assiduous details that distil the apartheid story.
263 and 344 Victoria Road

The Spa House

Contemporary residential architecture in Cape Town is superlative – there's plenty of talent, space and cash to play with here. A passion for linear forms and imaginative rationalism is entrenched, exemplified by this 2010 rentable three-bedroom villa by Jon Jacobson of Metropolis Design, which overlooks Hout Bay from a craggy vantage point. The steel-and-wood hideaway was conceived as a series of interlocking cubes floating over a waterscape, and cleverly hides its structural supports, resulting in an extraordinarily translucent structure. Set below the pool deck is an 'underwater' spa, offering views of flapping legs through its three expansive windows. Jacobson also devised nearby boutique wine farm Beau Constantia (T 021 794 8632), which centres around a delightful glass-box restaurant.
18 Avenue Suzanne, T 071 592 6787

Mutual Building

When completed in 1940, this 84m-high (91.4m with spire) masterpiece was hyped as 'the tallest building in Africa – after the pyramids'. A late example of art deco, it may lack the pizzazz of the Chrysler in New York, partly due to the low-rent neighbours that hem it in, but it has its own distinctive attributes. As well as the ziggurat design and the triangular window bays, check out the nine sculptural busts and the 118m-long carved-stone frieze that wraps round three sides of the base and depicts the history of settlers in southern Africa. The tower's prominence was short-lived – by the 1960s, insurer Old Mutual had started to relocate to the suburbs. However, it was repurposed into flats in 2005 by Louis Karol and Robert Silke, and the entrance still shimmers with the original veined black onyx and gold leaf.
14 Darling Street, T 021 465 6377

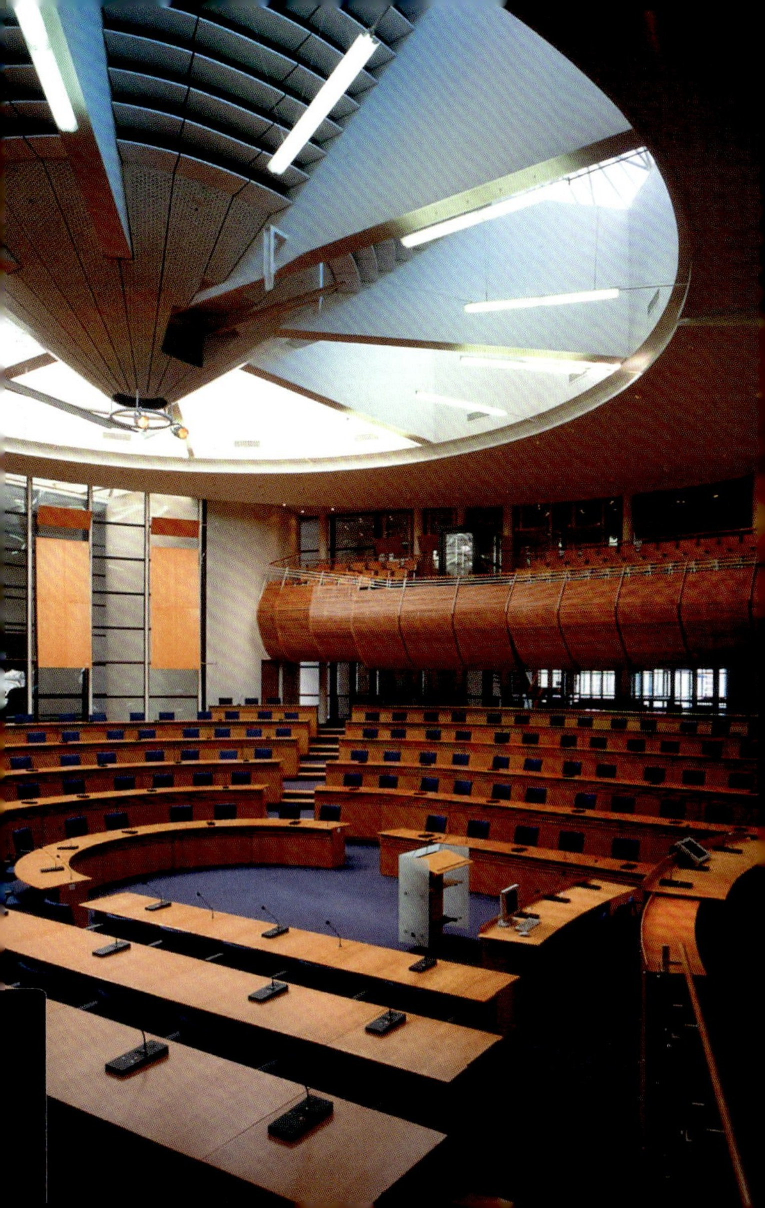

Civic Centre

Naudé, Papendorf, Van der Merwe and Meiring's 1978 Civic Centre – a brutalist concrete-and-glass block, 98m tall and twice as long, with a low podium building in front of it – was not the most obvious choice for the home of the newly unified city government in 2000. But the podium was expertly renovated by local architects KrugerRoos, who added an upper level to create a structure that's all about light and openness, and glass is used extensively to emphasise the transparency of civic duty. The inverted steel cone forming the roof of the council chamber (opposite) symbolises a fresh start, and acts as a wind disperser and shading device. It also contributes to the acoustics and changes colour with the weather. It is not, as some observers first thought, scaffolding that got left behind.
12 Hertzog Boulevard, T 086 010 3089

SHOPS
THE BEST RETAIL THERAPY AND WHAT TO BUY

De Waterkant's lifestyle emporiums and Kloof Street's independent fashion boutiques, typified by AKJP Studio (opposite) and Stefania Morland (153a Kloof Street, T 021 422 2609), known for combining natural fabrics with unique silhouettes, are a moocher's paradise, full of charming one-offs. Driving inner-city revival is Klûk CGDT (43-45 Bree Street, T 083 377 7780), offering South African couture. Modish stores also cluster around the junction of Church and Long Streets, such as Mememe (117a Long Street, T 021 424 0001), which carries classic womenswear, and it's worth seeking out Missibaba (229 Bree Street, T 021 424 8127) for leather accessories. CBD anchor Merchants on Long (see p092) is an institution; pick up an original scent by Frazer Parfum in a handblown glass flacon by David Reade.

Plenty of venues stock the work of local designers and makers, whose studios can be visited too. The bulk are found in Woodstock, Salt River and Observatory, notably Wiid Design (15 Baker Street, T 021 447 2512) and metal artisan Conrad Hicks (178 Lower Main Road, T 083 233 3083). Treats at The Woodstock Exchange (66-68 Albert Road, T 021 486 5999) include the furniture showrooms of Saks Corner (T 021 447 2966) and Pedersen + Lennard (T 021 447 2770). On Saturdays in this creative 'hood, The Neighbourgoods Market at The Old Biscuit Mill (373 Albert Road, T 021 447 8194) purveys homegrown micro fashion labels next to organic produce. *For full addresses, see Resources.*

AKJP Studio

Keith Henning launched streetwear label Adriaan Kuiters, named after his grandad, in 2012, and two years later a collaboration with artist Jody Paulsen, known for his felt tapestries in vivid colours with cheeky pop-culture references, led to the birth of AKJP. Signature pieces, such as appliquéd coats, overlong shirts and print dresses, feature arty twists on classic and unisex utilitarian ready-to-wear, cut into boxy silhouettes and incorporating vibrant patterns, layering and asymmetrical details. In his boutique, Henning also carries a whole coterie of South African brands: ruched dresses from W35T by Nicola West; leather bags and accessories by Thalia Strates; Githan Coopoo's ceramic jewellery, inspired by Jean Arp; and Ben Orkin's clay vessels.
73 Kloof Street, T 021 424 5502, www.akjpstudio.com

Skoon
After working with a chemist to synthesise plant oils, nut butters, floral essences and botanical extracts, Stella Ciolli founded her skincare brand in 2015. Its name, Afrikaans for 'clean', and pared-back packaging by native studio Grand Central, reflect its use of natural, non-toxic ingredients, including mastic gum, frangipani flowers, squalane, manuka honey and South African 'miracle herb' buchu. 'The One' super-moisturiser (above, R695) is made with oil from the indigenous marula fruit, an antioxidant, and organic rooibos extracts, while the 'Papaya + Pineapple' exfoliating mask mixes the enzymes found in these fruits (papain and bromelain) with clay. The range is available at the city's Wellness Warehouse outlets – the flagship branch is on Kloof Street (T 021 487 5420).
www.skoonskin.co.za

Dear Rae

Jeweller (and surfer) Karin Rae Matthee was raised in Cape Town and Betty's Bay, and launched Dear Rae from her parents' garage in 2010. She set up in Woodstock a year later, in a salesroom/studio (above) with items displayed in glass cloches and wood printers' trays, before moving to a similarly styled showroom on Bree Street in 2019. Her coastal upbringing continues to influence the designs, evident in the shell-inspired 'Ode to the Ocean' range and 'Life of Pi' rings, while coloured diamonds are a signature. Also browse Katherine-Mary Pichulik's booth at the Watershed market (T 021 408 7600) for accessories with a bolder African accent: handcrafted jewellery, and pieces made from found materials, rope, stone, glass and brass.
164 Bree Street, T 021 447 1390, www.dearrae.co.za

Merchants on Long
Behind an art nouveau terracotta facade, Hanneli Rupert's emporium is a treasure trove of African fashion and accessories. Displayed within a cave-like space, with slate walls and timber beams, seasonal collections include Xhosa beadwork-inspired knitwear by Laduma Ngxokolo, floral prints from Sindiso Khumalo and leather purses by in-house brand Okapi.
34 Long Street, T 021 422 2828

SHOPS

Andile Dyalvane
With their unmistakably southern African aesthetic, Andile Dyalvane's unique objects are another impressive facet of the roster at Southern Guild (see p068). These are glorious, one-off, super-sized statement pieces in terracotta clay ('Idladla', above); mainly decorative sculptures, although a few could function as furniture. Dyalvane also runs Imiso, which loosely translates as 'working today for a better tomorrow', with textile designer Zizipho Poswa. The studio infuses its functional ceramics with the Xhosa heritage of their makers. The 'Scarified' series references body-scarring practices used to mark life's milestones: incisions in the surface of the vases reveal blood-red clay underneath, or black oxide representing a healer's herb mixture.
Unit A102, The Old Biscuit Mill,
T 021 447 2627, www.imisoceramics.co.za

Loading Bay
Although Cape Town likes to foreground its European heritage, it often shares more of a kinship with west coast USA, especially in its brashness, which extends to its fashion sensibilities. Similar in ethos to Fred Segal in LA, Loading Bay makes a bold stand for stylish male apparel. The essence of the dapper brands on offer here, among them Norse Projects, Our Legacy, Acne Studios and Yoshida & Co, is tailored simplicity in functional, well-made garments; this in a city that still venerates surf baggies. The split-level, triple-volume space features raw concrete, white subway tiles and oak fixtures and fittings, and a café serves an all-day menu – fill up on spiced buckwheat and pumpkin-seed pancakes. Sister store Sans (see p062) stocks local homewares.
30 Hudson Street, T 021 425 6320, www.loadingbay.co.za

ESCAPES

WHERE TO GO IF YOU WANT TO LEAVE TOWN

It is by no means essential to leave Cape Town to get away from it all. There are beaches aplenty and some of South Africa's most dramatic topography right in the middle of the city. However, the coastal regions and hinterland to the north-east offer a bounty of adventure, wildlife and culinary delights. Although the Western Cape was heavily farmed for two centuries, conservationists have reintroduced 'big five' game – lion, elephant, leopard, buffalo and the endangered rhino – to their former habitat. There are upscale options, such as Aquila Private Game Reserve (R46, T 021 430 7260) in the southern Karoo, and Gondwana (6520 Mossel Bay, T 021 555 0807), a fynbos (shrubland) safari park where living quarters with round thatched roofs evoke traditional Khoisan architecture and overlook the valley waterholes. It's a six-hour drive from Cape Town, part of it on the R62, a legendary back road that winds up mountain passes and offers super panoramas. Thrill-seekers should continue east along the Garden Route, glorious in spring, to bungee jump from Africa's highest single-span concrete-arch bridge (6600 Tsitsikamma, T 042 281 1458), 40km east of Plettenberg Bay.

Much closer to Cape Town, Franschhoek, about 75km away, is known for its cuisine, including La Petite Colombe (opposite) and Chris Erasmus' Foliage (11 Huguenot Road, T 021 876 2328), as well as its Gallic history (Franschhoek translates as 'French corner'). *For full addresses, see Resources.*

La Petite Colombe, Franschhoek

Settled by Huguenot refugees in the late 17th century, many of whom were experts in viticulture and oenology, Franschhoek is famous for its vineyards and grand Cape Dutch farmhouses, and has turned into a billionaires' playground. A 2010 vacation brought Indian businessman Analjit Singh to the area and his portfolio now includes Leeu Estates (T 021 492 2222), a 17-room mansion with winery and spa, and bijou hotel Le Quartier Français (T 021 876 2151), where this offshoot of chef Scot Kirton's La Colombe (see p040) is set. The Gourmand menu features dishes like sea bass, squid, parsnip, mussel, leeks and chorizo, paired with Paulina's Reserve semillon from local label Rickety Bridge. The styling is modern country; aim for a spot in the conservatory.
Berg Street/Wilhelmina Street,
T 021 202 3395, www.lapetitecolombe.com

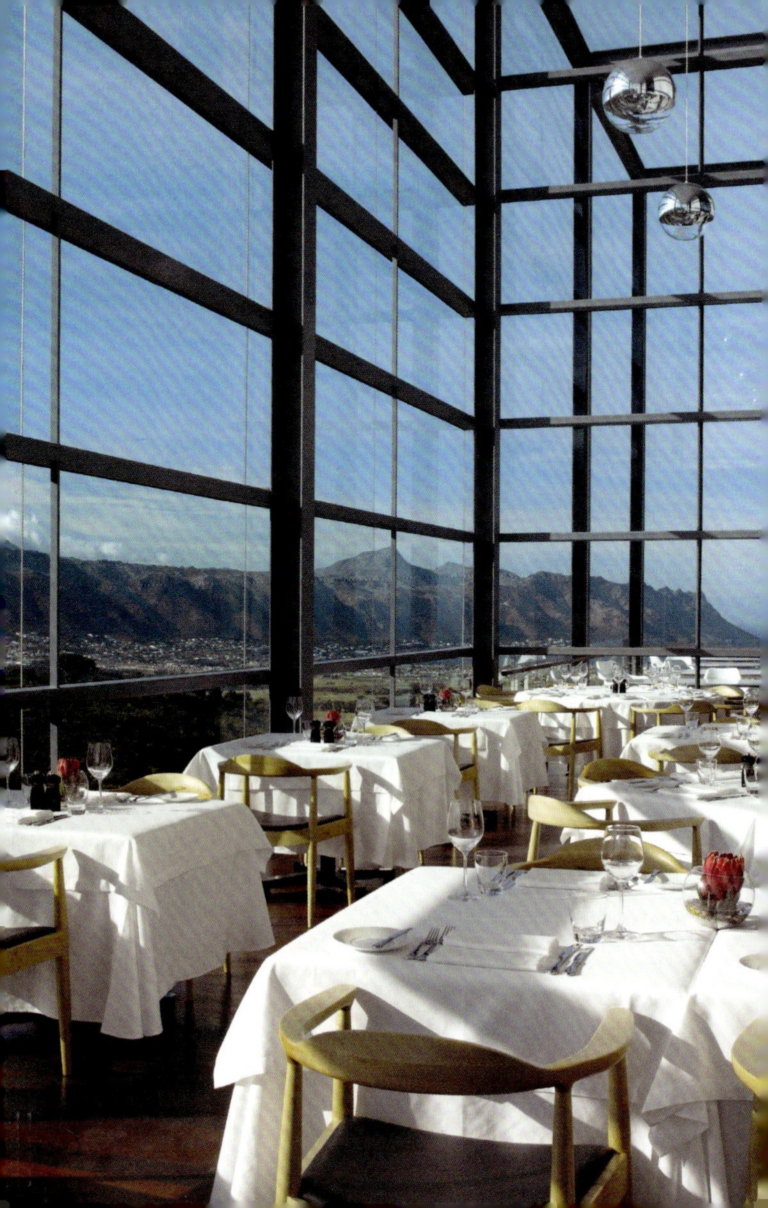

Waterkloof

The fussy Gallic yearnings and gabled vernacular of the Cape's older wine farms have been wilfully disregarded since the millennium, and Waterkloof gleefully flouts tradition. Located on Schapenberg ridge above False Bay, flanked by biodynamic vineyards, this dramatic 'cellar in the sky' is distinctive for a glass-and-steel box that cantilevers out of the off-shutter concrete facade. It houses French chef Gregory Czarnecki's vogueish restaurant, which has interiors by Frank Böhm; the iron tree in the grounds is by Strijdom van der Merwe. The estate is known for its sauvignon blanc and also produces a lively cinsault. Tokara (see p024) in Stellenbosch, which features Marco Cianfanelli's 'windswept' sculptures, was a big player in this design renaissance.
Sir Lowry's Pass Road, Somerset West, T 021 858 1292, www.waterkloofwines.co.za

Babylonstoren, Paarl

Set in the Drakenstein Valley, a 45-minute drive from Cape Town, Babylonstoren and its restaurant Babel is a must for foodies. The Cape Dutch homestead looks much as it did in 1777, but for the stylish interiors by designer Karen Roos. The focal point of the estate is an ordered garden with more than 300 varieties of edible plants. You'll also find beehives, a prickly pear maze, a vineyard producing nine wines, and the lovely balauwood Puff Adder walk (above), devised by Patrice Taravella and Terry de Waal. Diners can pick their own food but book well in advance for lunch or supper; casual visitors can eat in the Greenhouse. The hotel is fastidiously white, rooms have open-hearth fires, and there's a bamboo-clad spa. It's less busy early in the summer.
Klapmuts to Simondium Road,
T 021 863 3852, www.babylonstoren.com

Wolfgat, West Coast Peninsula

Set in an 1880s whitewashed cottage and named after a cave on the premises that was used by the hyenas that roamed these beaches (and which has also yielded First People finds), Wolfgat is the domain of chef Kobus van der Merwe. He earnt his stripes running his parents' nearby bistro Oep ve Koep (T 022 752 2033) and specialises in hyper-local cuisine showcasing ingredients foraged from coastal pools and endemic *veldkos* in a seven-course menu. Unusual, imaginative dishes, such as Saldanha Bay mussels with dune celery and cauliflower, oysters draped in *soutslaai* (a succulent) with gooseberries, and rooibos-smoked angelfish, reward the 160km drive north. In keeping with the venue's carnivorous name, local lamb and venison feature too.
*10 Sampson Street, Paternoster,
www.wolfgat.co.za*

Bosjes, Breede Valley
Amid dramatic scenery 90 minutes from the city, this divine retreat is set on 300 hectares of cultivable land, comprising vineyards, fynbos, and olive and peach orchards. An 18th-century barn has been converted into a five-suite guesthouse by TV3, Town Planners and designer Liam Mooney, who has given it an interior that mirrors the hues of the terroir, with oak furnishings and chartreuse accents. In the grounds, Steyn Studio's lovely chapel (pictured) has a concrete waveform roof that appears to float on a reflective pool and evokes the mountain ranges in the distance. At restaurant Bosjes Kombuis, Lourens Engelbrecht's seasonal dishes pair beautifully with the house wines; we recommend Allan Mullins' chenin blanc blend from the Breedekloof Valley.
R43, T 023 004 0496, www.bosjes.co.za

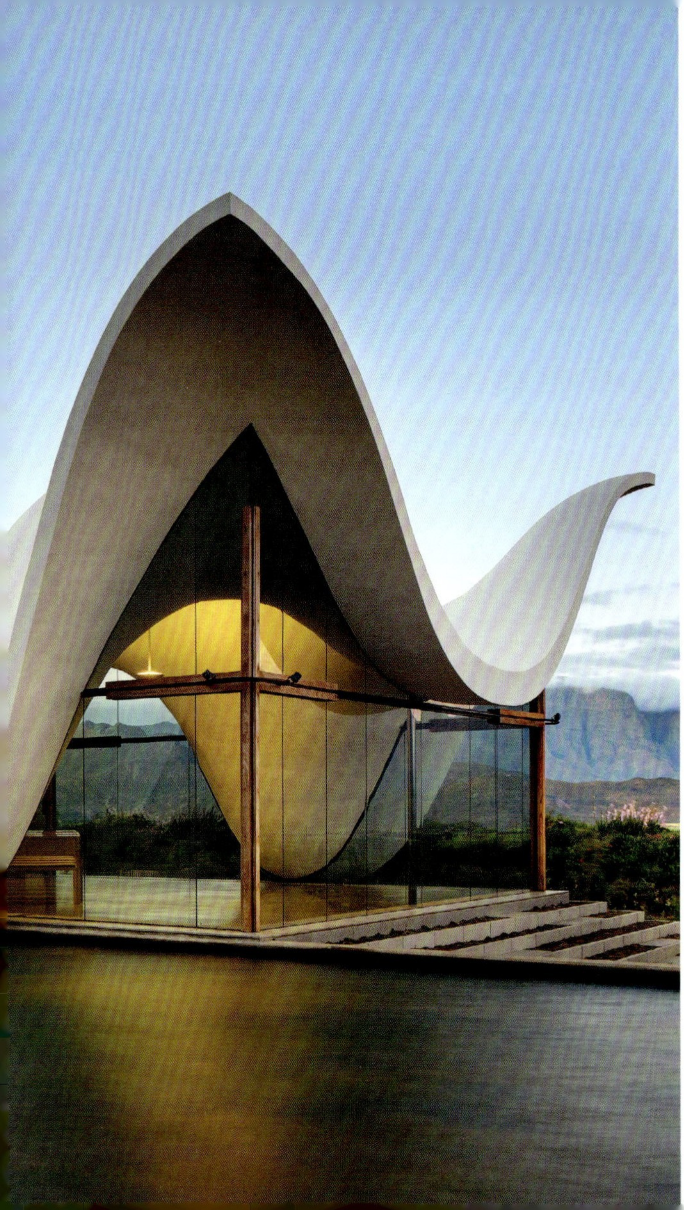

Wallpaper*
City Guide

50 CITIES NOW AVAILABLE IN ONE APP

Your passport to global style

Download digital guides for Android and Apple phones and tablets in one container app via
www.phaidon.com/wcg

NOTES
SKETCHES AND MEMOS

RESOURCES
CITY GUIDE DIRECTORY

A
A4 Arts Foundation 079
23 Buitenkant Street
T 010 880 2595
www.a4arts.org

AKJP Studio 089
73 Kloof Street
T 021 424 5502
www.akjpstudio.com

Atang Tshikare 071
www.atangtshikare.com

The Athletic Club & Social 062
35 Buitengracht Street
T 021 012 5331
www.theathletic.co.za

Aubergine 024
39 Barnet Street
T 021 465 0000
www.aubergine.co.za

AVA 078
35 Church Street
T 021 424 7436
www.ava.co.za

B
Baxter Theatre Centre 036
Main Road
Rondebosch
T 021 685 7880
www.baxter.co.za

Beau Constantia 084
1043 Constantia Main Road
Constantia
T 021 794 8632
www.beauconstantia.com

Between Us 026
176 Bree Street
T 021 823 8695
www.betweenus.capetown

The Black Sheep 051
104 Kloof Street
T 021 426 2661
www.blacksheeprestaurant.co.za

Blank Projects 075
10 Lewin Street
T 021 462 4276
www.blankprojects.com

Bloukrans Bridge 096
6600 Tsitsikamma
Bloukrans
T 042 281 1458
www.faceadrenalin.com

Bronze Age 064
1b Coode Crescent
T 021 421 2223
www.bronzeage.co.za

El Burro 060
81 Main Road
T 021 433 2364
www.elburro.co.za

El Burro Taqueria 060
12-16 Kloof Nek Road
T 021 433 3554

C
Cabrito 060
81 Main Road
T 021 433 2364
www.elburro.co.za

Cape Capers 076
20 Erica Street
T 021 448 3117
www.tourcapers.co.za

Cape Town Stadium 014
Fritz Sonnenberg Road

Carne SA 052
70 Keerom Street
T 021 424 3460
153 Kloof Street
T 021 426 5566
www.carne-sa.com
Castle of Good Hope 009
Castle Street/Darling Street
T 021 787 1260
Centenary Tree Canopy Walkway 081
Kirstenbosch National Botanical Garden
Rhodes Drive
Newlands
T 021 799 8800
www.sanbi.org/gardens/kirstenbosch
Chefs Warehouse & Canteen 024
92 Bree Street
T 021 422 0128
www.chefswarehouse.co.za
Civic Centre 086
12 Hertzog Boulevard
T 086 010 3089
Clarke's Bar & Dining Room 055
133 Bree Street
T 087 470 0165
www.clarkesdining.co.za
La Colombe 040
Silvermist Wine Estate
Main Road
Constantia
T 021 794 2390
www.lacolombe.co.za
The Company's Garden Restaurant 024
15 Queen Victoria Street
T 021 423 2919
www.thecompanysgarden.com

Conrad Hicks 088
178 Lower Main Road
T 083 233 3083
www.conradhicks.com
Customs House 080
Heerengracht Street

D
Daor Contemporary 069
Coode Crescent
T 021 001 2633
www.daor.co.za
The Dark Horse 062
145 Kloof Street
T 021 422 0825
www.darkhorsebar.co.za
Dear Rae 091
164 Bree Street
T 021 447 1390
www.dearrae.co.za
Delaire Graff Estate 034
R310
Helshoogte Pass
Stellenbosch
T 021 885 8160
www.delaire.co.za
Disa Park Towers 010
Chelmsford Road

E
Ebony/Curated 070
67 Loop Street
T 021 424 9985
4 Franschhoek Square
Huguenot Street
Franschhoek
T 021 876 4477
www.ebonydesign.co.za

Everard Read/CIRCA 074
3 Portswood Road
T 021 418 4527
www.everard-read-capetown.co.za

F
Faith XLVII mural 074
59 Philip Kgosana Drive
Zonnebloem
www.faith47.com
Foliage 096
11 Huguenot Road
Franschhoek
T 021 876 2328
www.foliage.co.za
Fork 051
84 Long Street
T 021 424 6334
www.fork-restaurants.co.za
The Fugard Theatre 037
Caledon Street
T 021 461 4554
www.thefugard.com

G
The Gin Bar 048
64a Wale Street
T 071 241 2277
www.theginbar.co.za
Giovanni's 014
103 Main Road
T 021 434 6893
Goodman Gallery 065
3rd floor
Fairweather House
176 Sir Lowry Road
T 021 462 7573
www.goodman-gallery.com

Grand Africa Café & Beach 047
1 Haul Road
T 071 382 7044
www.grandafrica.com
Greenhouse 054
The Cellars-Hohenort
93 Brommersvlei Road
T 021 795 6226
www.greenhouserestaurant.co.za
Guga S'Thebe 076
King Langalibalele Street/Church Street
Langa
T 021 695 3493

H
The Haas Collective 059
19 Buitenkant Street
T 021 461 1812
www.haascollective.com
Hank's Olde Irish 024
110 Bree Street
T 021 422 2770
www.hanks.co.za
Harbour House 058
1st floor
Kalk Bay Harbour
T 021 788 4136
www.harbourhouse.co.za
Hemelhuijs 046
71 Waterkant Street
T 021 418 2042
www.hemelhuijs.co.za
The Hussar Grill 040
108 Camps Bay Drive
T 021 438 0151
www.hussargrill.co.za

I
Imiso 094
Unit A102
The Old Biscuit Mill
373-375 Albert Road
T 021 447 2627
www.imisoceramics.co.za

K
The Kitchen 031
111-113 Sir Lowry Road
T 021 462 2201
www.lovethekitchen.co.za
Klûk CGDT 088
43-45 Bree Street
T 083 377 7780
www.klukcgdt.com
Kyoto Garden Japanese Restaurant 043
11 Kloof Nek Road
T 021 422 2001
www.kyotogarden.co.za

L
Loading Bay 095
30 Hudson Street
T 021 425 6320
www.loadingbay.co.za

M
Maitland Institute 064
372 Voortrekker Road
www.maitlandinstitute.com
Margot Molyneux 062
69 Roeland Street
T 021 461 4565
www.margotmolyneux.com

Mariendahl Brewery 083
3 Main Road
Newlands
T 021 658 7440
www.newlandsbrewery.co.za
Mason's Press 064
7 Ravenscraig Road
T 021 424 1210
Mememe 088
117a Long Street
T 021 424 0001
www.mememe.co.za
Merchants On Long 092
34 Long Street
T 021 422 2828
www.merchantsonlong.com
Missibaba 088
229 Bree Street
T 021 424 8127
www.missibaba.com
Momo 064
16 Buiten Street
T 021 424 5140
www.gallerymomo.com
The Moveable Feast 043
13 Kloof Nek Road
T 087 897 9749
www.themoveablefeast.co.za
Mulberry & Prince 041
12 Pepper Street
T 021 422 3301
www.mulberryandprince.co.za
Mutual Building 085
14 Darling Street
T 021 465 6377

N

95 Keerom 052
*95 Keerom Street
T 021 422 0765
www.95keerom.com*

Naspers Centre 080
40 Heerengracht Street

The Neighbourgoods Market 088
*The Old Biscuit Mill
373-375 Albert Road
www.neighbourgoodsmarket.co.za*

Newlands Swimming Pool 027
*Main Road/Sans Souci Road
T 021 671 2729*

Norval Foundation 072
*4 Steenberg Road
T 087 654 5900
www.norvalfoundation.org*

O

Oep ve Koep 101
*St Augustine Road
Paternoster
T 022 752 2033
www.oepvekoep.co.za*

Okha 071
*109 Hatfield Street
T 021 461 7233
www.okha.com*

The Old Biscuit Mill 088
*373-375 Albert Road
T 021 447 8194
www.theoldbiscuitmill.co.za*

Olive Branch Deli 062
*50 Kloof Street
T 073 847 5499
www.olivebranchdeli.com*

Olympia Café 040
*134 Main Road
Kalk Bay
T 021 788 6396
www.olympiacafe.co.za*

Open House 066
Long Street/Dorp Street

Orphanage Cocktail Emporium 024
*227 Bree Street
T 071 534 0266
www.orphanageclub.co.za*

P

Pedersen + Lennard 088
*The Woodstock Exchange
66 Albert Road
T 021 447 2770
www.pedersenlennard.co.za*

Peppertree Café 025
*94 Kloof Street
T 021 424 5540*

La Perla 040
*209 Beach Road
T 021 439 9538
www.laperla.co.za*

La Petite Colombe 097
*Berg Street/Wilhelmina Street
Franschhoek
T 021 202 3395
www.lapetitecolombe.com*

Pichulik 091
*F36/F37
Watershed
Dock Road
www.pichulik.com*

The Pot Luck Club 038
6th floor
The Old Biscuit Mill
373-375 Albert Road
T 021 447 0804
www.thepotluckclub.co.za
The Power & The Glory 043
Kloof Nek Road/Burnside Road
T 021 422 2108

R
Railway Station 080
Adderley Street
T 080 065 6463
Reuben's Restaurant & Bar 040
2 Daniel Hugo Street
Franschhoek
T 021 876 3772
www.reubens.co.za
Rex Trueform 082
263 and 344 Victoria Road
Salt River
www.rextrueform.co.za
Ritz Hotel 013
Main Road/Camberwell Road
Royale Eatery 060
273 Long Street
T 021 422 4536
www.royaleeatery.com

S
SABC 027
209 St James Road
St George's Cathedral 024
5 Wale Street
T 021 424 7360
www.sgcathedral.co.za

Saks Corner 088
The Woodstock Exchange
66 Albert Road
T 021 447 2966
www.sakscorner.co.za
Salsify at The Roundhouse 056
1 Roundhouse Road
off Kloof Road
T 021 010 6444
www.salsify.co.za
Sans 062
277 Main Road
T 021 205 4555
www.sanscommunity.com
Sea Point Pavilion 027
Beach Road
T 021 434 3341
The Sidewalk Café 011
33 Derry Street
T 021 461 2839
www.sidewalk.co.za
Skinny Legs 026
70 Loop Street
T 021 423 5403
www.skinnylegscafe.co.za
Skoon 090
www.skoonskin.co.za
SMAC 064
145 Sir Lowry Road
T 021 461 1029
www.smacgallery.com
Smith 078
56 Church Street
T 021 422 0814
www.smithstudio.co.za
Societi Bistro 040
50 Orange Street
T 021 424 2100
www.societi.co.za

South African National Gallery 028
Government Avenue
Company's Garden
T 021 481 3970
www.iziko.org.za
Southern Guild 068
Shop 5b
Silo 5
T 021 461 2856
www.southernguild.co.za
The Spa House 084
18 Avenue Suzanne
T 071 592 6787
Stefania Morland 088
153a Kloof Street
T 021 422 2609
www.stefaniamorland.com
Stevenson 065
Buchanan Building
160 Sir Lowry Road
T 021 462 1500
www.stevenson.info
Superette 061
The Woodstock Exchange
66 Albert Road
T 021 802 5525
www.superette.co.za
Swan Café 044
Buitenkant/Barrack Street
T 079 454 4758
www.swancafe.co.za

T
236 Buitengracht Street 080
www.teamarchitects.co.za
Taal Monument 032
Gabbema Doordrift Street
Paarl Mountain
T 021 863 4809
www.taalmuseum.co.za

Table Mountain Aerial Cableway 025
Lower Cableway Station
Tafelberg Road
T 021 424 8181
www.tablemountain.net
The Test Kitchen 050
The Old Biscuit Mill
373-375 Albert Road
T 021 447 2337
www.thetestkitchen.co.za
La Tête 042
17 Bree Street
T 021 418 1299
www.latete.co.za
Tiger's Milk 058
Main Road
Kalk Bay
T 021 286 6805
www.tigersmilk.co.za
Tjing Tjing 039
165 Longmarket Street
T 021 422 4920
www.tjingtjing.co.za
Tokara 024
Helshoogte Pass
Stellenbosch
T 021 808 5900
www.tokararestaurant.co.za
The Twelve Apostles Spa 035
The Twelve Apostles Hotel
Victoria Road
T 021 437 9060
www.12apostleshotel.com

V
Van Hunks 039
Kloof Street/Upper Union Street
T 021 422 5422
www.vanhunks.co.za

W

Waterkloof 098
*Sir Lowry's Pass Road
Somerset West
T 021 858 1292
www.waterkloofwines.co.za*

Wellness Warehouse 090
*50 Kloof Street
T 021 487 5420
www.wellnesswarehouse.com*

Werdmuller Centre 080
*Main Road
Claremont*

Whatiftheworld 067
*16 Buiten Street
T 021 422 1066
www.whatiftheworld.com*

Wiid Design 088
*15 Baker Street
Observatory
T 021 447 2512
www.wiiddesign.co.za*

Wolfgat 101
*10 Sampson Street
Paternoster
West Coast Peninsula
www.wolfgat.co.za*
Reservation only. Lunch is served at 12.30pm, Wednesday to Saturday, and 12pm on Sunday; dinner at 6.30pm on Fridays and Saturdays

The Woodstock Exchange 064
*66-68 Albert Road
T 021 486 5999
www.woodstockexchange.co.za*

Z

Zeitz MOCAA 030
*Silo District
S Arm Road
T 087 350 4777
www.zeitzmocaa.museum*

ZerO21 Social Club 062
*46 Canterbury Street
T 071 760 3178
www.zer021.co.za*

HOTELS
ADDRESSES AND ROOM RATES

Aquila Private Game Reserve 096
Room rates:
double, from R1,900 (per person)
R46
T 021 430 7260
www.aquilasafari.com

Babylonstoren 100
Room rates:
double, from R6,600
Klapmuts to Simondium Road
Paarl
T 021 863 3852
www.babylonstoren.com

Belmond Mount Nelson Hotel 016
Room rates:
double, from R4,700
76 Orange Street
T 021 483 1000
www.mountnelson.co.za

Bosjes 103
Room rates:
double, from R2,750
R43
Breede Valley
T 023 004 0496
www.bosjes.co.za

Camps Bay Retreat 018
Room rates:
double, from R2,000;
Room One, prices on request
7 Chilworth Road
T 021 437 8300
www.campsbayretreat.com

Cape Grace 016
Room rates:
double, from R8,100
West Quay Road
T 021 410 7100
www.capegrace.com

Ellerman House 019
Room rates:
double, from R10,000;
Villa Two, from R75,000;
Villa One, from R85,000
180 Kloof Road
T 021 430 3200
www.ellerman.co.za

Glen Beach Bungalow 016
Room rates:
The Penthouse, from R4,000
12 Glen Beach
Victoria Road
T 083 675 8266
www.glenbeachvillas.co.za

Gondwana 096
Room rates:
Kwena Lodge, from R5,700
6520 Mossel Bay
Mossel Bay
T 021 555 0807
www.gondwanagr.co.za

Gorgeous George 017
Room rates:
Studio, from R2,000
118 St George's Mall
T 087 898 6000
www.gorgeousgeorge.co.za

Kensington Place 022
Room rates:
double, from R3,400
38 Kensington Crescent
T 021 424 4744
www.kensingtonplace.co.za

Leeu Estates 097
Room rates:
double, from R10,700
Dassenberg Road
Franschhoek
T 021 492 2222
www.leeucollection.com

The Marly 016
Room rates:
Suite, from R2,000
201 Victoria Road
T 021 437 1287
www.themarly.co.za

POD 020
Room rates:
double, from R3,550;
Deluxe Suite, from R8,400
3 Argyle Street
T 021 438 8550
www.pod.co.za

Le Quartier Français 097
Room rates:
double, from R7,700
Berg Street/Wilhelmina Street
Franschhoek
T 021 876 2151
www.leeucollection.com

The Silo 016
Room rates:
double, from R13,500
S Arm Road
Silo Square
Silo District
T 021 670 0500
www.theroyalportfolio.com/the-silo

The Tree House Boutique Hotel 023
Room rates:
Sea View Room, from R2,550;
Super Mountain Room, from R3,150
28 Vesperdene Road
T 021 439 9296
www.thetreehouseboutiquehotel.co.za

2inn1 Kensington 016
Room rates:
double, from R2,900
21 Kensington Crescent
T 021 423 1707
www.2inn1.com

21 Nettleton 016
Room rates:
Suite, from R11,000
21 Nettleton Road
T 021 438 1122
www.21nettleton.com

26 Sunset Villa 016
Room rates:
Suite, prices on request
26 Sunset Avenue
Llandudno
T 082 826 9986
www.26sunsetvilla.com

WALLPAPER* CITY GUIDES

Executive Editor
Jeremy Case

Author
Sean O'Toole

Photography Editor
Rebecca Moldenhauer

Art Editor
Jade R Arroyo

Senior Sub-Editor
Sean McGeady

Editorial Assistant
Josh Lee

Contributor
Bridget Downing

Interns
Daniela Duhur
Eva Clifford

Cape Town Imprint
First published 2007
Fifth edition 2019

ISBN 978 0 7148 7904 8

More City Guides
www.phaidon.com/travel

Follow us
@wallpaperguides

Contact
wcg@phaidon.com

Original Design
Loran Stosskopf

Map Illustrator
Russell Bell

Production Controller
Gif Jittiwutikarn

Assistant Production Controller
Lily Rodgers

Wallpaper* Magazine
161 Marsh Wall
London E14 9AP
contact@wallpaper.com

Wallpaper*® is a registered trademark of TI Media

Phaidon Press Limited
Regent's Wharf
All Saints Street
London N1 9PA

Phaidon Press Inc
65 Bleecker Street
New York, NY 10012

All prices and venue information are correct at time of going to press, but are subject to change.

A CIP Catalogue record for this book is available from the British Library.

All rights reserved. No part of this publication may be reproduced, stored in a retrieval system or transmitted, in any form or by any means, electronic, mechanical, photocopying, recording or otherwise, without the prior permission of Phaidon Press.

Phaidon® is a registered trademark of Phaidon Press Limited

© Phaidon Press Limited

PHOTOGRAPHERS

Jac de Villiers
Cape Town city view, inside front cover
Disa Park Towers, pp010-011
Ritz Hotel, p013
Gorgeous George, p017
Camps Bay Retreat, p018
Ellerman House, p019
Kensington Place, p022
Between Us, p026
Sea Point Pavilion, p027
South African National Gallery, pp028-029
Zeitz MOCAA, p030
The Twelve Apostles Spa, p035
The Pot Luck Club, p038, p039
Mulberry & Prince, p041
La Tête, p042
The Moveable Feast, p043
Swan Café, p044, p045
Hemelhuijs, p046
The Gin Bar, pp048-049
The Test Kitchen, p050
The Black Sheep, p051
Carne SA, pp052-053
Greenhouse, p054
Clarke's Bar & Dining Room, p055
Salsify at The Roundhouse, p056, p057
Harbour House, p058
The Haas Collective, p059
El Burro Taqueria, p060
Superette, p061
Marsi van de Heuvel, p063
Open House, p066
Ebony/Curated, p070
Norval Foundation, p073
Faith XLVII, p074
Blank Projects, p075
Centenary Tree Canopy Walkway, p081
Rex Trueform, pp082-083
The Spa House, p084
Mutual Building, p085
Civic Centre, p087
AKJP Studio, p089
Dear Rae, p091
Merchants on Long, pp092-093
Loading Bay, p095
Wolfgat, p101

Susan Bockelmann and Dennis Gilbert
Cape Town Stadium, pp014-015
The Kitchen, p031
Stevenson, p065

Wianélle Briers
Zeitz MOCAA, p012

Christopher Floyd
Taal Monument, pp032-033

Claire Gunn
La Petite Colombe, p097

Adam Letch
Bosjes, pp102-103

Adriaan Louw
Andile Dyalvane, p094

Kate McLuckie
Southern Guild, pp068-069

Kyle Morland
A4 Arts Foundation, p079

Hayden Phipps
Whatiftheworld, p067
Atang Tshikare, p071

Alain Proust
Babylonstoren, p100

Karl Rogers
Norval Foundation, p072

David Southwood
Table Mountain, p025
Guga S'Thebe, pp076-077

Jonathan de Villiers
Baxter Theatre Centre, pp036-037

CAPE TOWN
A COLOUR-CODED GUIDE TO THE HOT 'HOODS

ATLANTIC SEABOARD
Designer homes and lively bars and eateries nestle between the mountains and the ocean

GREEN POINT
The epicentre of redevelopment for the World Cup boasts much more than its stadium

CENTRE
Long Street is the city's main drag but Bree Street's boutiques and cafés will draw you back

WATERFRONT/LOWER CITY
The slick V&A marina is a tourist magnet; the architecture of the CBD is more interesting

WOODSTOCK
Art galleries and independent retail have transformed a sketchy area into a creative hub

CITY BOWL SUBURBS
Sought-after real estate spreads out from Kloof Street's upmarket stores and nightlife

For a full description of each neighbourhood, see the Introduction.
Featured venues are colour-coded, according to the district in which they are located.